Goodnight Ballivor,
I'll Sleep in Trim

A CHILDHOOD MEMOIR

JOHN QUINN

Goodnight Ballivor, I'll Sleep in Trim

A CHILDHOOD MEMOIR

VERITAS

First published 2008 by
Veritas Publications
7/8 Lower Abbey Street
Dublin 1
Ireland
Email publications@veritas.ie
Website www.veritas.ie

ISBN 978 1 84730 100 0

Extracts from *The Summer of Lily and Esme* (1991) and *Generations of the Moon*
(1995) by John Quinn, courtesy of Poolbeg Press. The final two lines of 'The One' by
Patrick Kavanagh are reprinted from *Collected Poems*, edited by Antoinette Quinn
(Allen Lane, 2004), by kind permission of the Trustees of the Estate of the late
Katherine B. Kavanagh, through the Jonathan Williams Literary Agency. Extract from
Memoir by John McGahern, courtesy of Faber, 2005. Extract from *How Green was my
Valley* by Richard Llewellyn, courtesy of Scribner, 1997. Extract from *The Quiet
Revolution: The Electrification of Rural Ireland 1946–1976* by Michael Shiel, courtesy
of O'Brien Press, 2003.

Designed by Colette Dower
Cover photograph, Detail of Main Street, Ballivor village, 1994,
courtesy of Marie McClair
Printed in the Republic of Ireland by ColourBooks Ltd, Dublin

*Veritas books are printed on paper made from the wood pulp of managed
forests. For every tree felled, at least one tree is planted, thereby renewing
natural resources.*

Dedicated
to the wonderful McGearty family
(especially to Maureen, the memory woman)
keepers of the faith, keepers of the record,
at the heart of Ballivor life
for a century.

Acknowledgements
Sincere thanks to the many people who have helped me in compiling this memoir:

- the McGearty family, especially Maureen, M.J., Josephine and Patsy
- Medhbh agus Eithne Ní Chonmhuidhe and their late mother, Margaret
- Padraig McGinn, formerly of the ESB
- Breda McLaughlin-Bligh
- the late Eilís Brady, folklorist
- my own siblings, Kay, Mary and Noel
- the late Jimmy Murray, musician and songster
- the balladeer Tom Kiernan
- the 'day on the bog' team, especially Joe Dempsey and the late Johnny Kelly and Frank Kelly
- Paddy 'Stonewall' Dixon
- all the residents of Ballivor, long departed, who contributed so much to my real education
- Marie Murray, for permission to quote from her *Irish Times* article and for her introduction to this book
- Máire Ní Fhrighil, who typed the manuscript so efficiently
- Marie McClair, Pat Donlon, the McGearty and Hiney families and Jim Dargan for photographs supplied
- Caitriona Clarke of Veritas for her much-valued editorial skills

Contents

Preface

Not another memoir of childhood? Well, yes actually. Not another regressive desire to capture a golden weren't-we-poor-but-happy age? Well, no. Nor a pursuit of dark and misery and repression either. This is simply a journey into my past in a quiet, sleepy midlands village. Of course it bears no relation to the Ballivor of the twenty-first century. How could it? Why should it? This memoir is simply stating that there was another Ballivor. This was how we lived sixty-odd years ago. It neither invites nor suggests comparison with the modern Ballivor. These are my memories and the collective memories of some of my contemporaries. I feel it is important to set them down in print so that my children and future generations will know the world from which they evolved.

This book grew out of the radio documentary *Goodnight Ballivor, I'll Sleep in Trim*. That expression, common to us in our childhood yet shrouded in mystery, was the obvious title to give to a radio memoir. The wonderful reaction to it surprised me, but it shouldn't have. It was the old story of the local being universal. A number of people suggested I should expand the story and transfer it to print. Twelve years later, I have acceded to their requests.

Writing the story was easy and was done with love and pride – and, yes, not a little nostalgia. The psychologist Marie Murray has written that nostalgia is a much-maligned emotion:

It is not mere regressive reminiscence. It is finely-tuned remembrance of the particular historical time in which a person lived out seminal years of life, time worth recording, events worth remembering, an era within an epoch etched into the annals of memory, the personal narrative rather than the archival records in the local museum. Visiting a place in which one was happy, remembering the details of an earlier time, retracing steps, noting differences wrought by time, imagining one's former self and that of others, yet recognising that this time is over, shows the courage to connect the past and the present and to value them both.

That will do for me. This is my 'personal narrative of time worth recording'. I hope my memory has not skewed the narrative in any way. If there are any misapprehensions or misinterpretations, they are entirely my fault. It is over fifty years since my family left Ballivor, yet I have always cherished it. The Greek poet Cavafy wrote:

In those fields and streets where you grew up, there you will always live and there you will die.

Amen. Marie Murray put it another way:

Home draws us. Didn't Odysseus, despite his voyages, his expeditions, the temptations of immortality, the possibility of having a life of luxury, despite peril and portents and the Siren's call, want to go home? And home he went.

This simple and straightforward story is my odyssey home.

JOHN QUINN
FEBRUARY 2008

Introduction

Social history is recorded by each of us as individuals, and collectively in our accounts to each other of our lives and the life of our times. In *Goodnight Ballivor, I'll Sleep in Trim*, John Quinn returns to his personal past and we accompany him on this special odyssey to a former era in Irish social history. It is a visit from which one emerges with remembrance or understanding of an age that has ended, a way of life that has ceased, roles that are defunct, services that are obsolete, practices that no longer exist and social customs, most of which would be incomprehensible to the current generation.

In the mid-twentieth century, societal structures, educational organisations, social behaviour, civil codes, interpersonal interactions, family size and composition, marital relationships, gender roles, sexual mores, child rearing customs, moral perspectives and religious practice were intimately tied to each other. How one lived one's life was, in many ways, pre-determined, predictable and reliable. As this book shows, life was filled with characters, places, activities and consciousness of the seasonality of happiness and sadness, loss and gain, life and death and an overriding belief in living the present and aspiring to eternal reward.

If you recognise this world, if it is within your living memory, then you are of a certain age and likely to be overwhelmed by the storehouse of recollections and resonances this book will evoke, for the story is beautifully told, vividly portrayed and meticulously documented. If this world is new to you, if it is not of your time or place, then it is a special opportunity and personal invitation into understanding a way of life that shaped the Irish psyche today. For *Goodnight Ballivor, I'll Sleep in Trim* preserves and renders permanent a particular part of our culture's past. It does so in the narrative tradition through which personal histories and cultural identities are formed. 'To give people back a memory,' says French philosopher Paul Ricoeur, 'is also to give them back a future.' This book acknowledges that. It recognises that if we do not know from whence we came, how we got there and where we are going, we cannot understand where we are now, what we are travelling towards and why. By setting down in print this perspective on the past, as the author himself says, 'future generations will know the world from which they evolved'.

This brings us to another important psychological function this book serves. It revisits a time about which the dominant discourse to date has, primarily, been one of oppressive poverty, appalling abuse, obsessive adherence to rules and blatant misuse of privilege and power. Constructed as a time of routine, state-sanctioned physical punishment of children in school and at home, of gross gender inequality with paradoxical idealisation of motherhood, suspicion of spinsterhood and misogynistic fear of the mysteries of womanhood, it was also distinguished by the quiet desperation of many men supporting large families or aging bachelors living alone, eking out an existence on isolated farmsteads.

These dimensions of the past cannot be denied, but there was also another softer, kinder, gentler, parallel world in which people lived out their lives then. There was compassion and humanity, concern for neighbours, respect for age, time to talk, midwives who delivered a village of children, teachers who educated them, parents who begat and did their best for them and a community that reared them.

This is an equally valid world that John Quinn recalls and narrates and one that has often been overlooked. It is a place in which a child was happy, where life was full of activity, yet there was time to amble, observe and mentally mooch, where treats were infrequent but appreciated and life was punctuated by school and home, fair day and threshing day, street games and religious rituals and visits to the cinema. John Quinn's world is peopled with characters: the sergeant, the grocer, the tailor and the master. It contains the objects of another time: the tilly lamp, canisters of milk, pictures of the Sacred Heart, bellows and washtubs, wet batteries and 'seven shillings and sixpence for footing a square of turf'. There were activities: opening a furrow, going to the privy, listening to the radio, saying the rosary, visiting 'the Big Smoke', having a turn at the churn and, most importantly, 'taking it nice and cushy' in a world that made time for people to spend time with each other. There were loving relationships: the longing of a little boy to live forever in the back kitchen with his mother and the aching, unspoken love of a son for a father whose presence and absence remain with him forever.

To revere the past and demonise the present, or to venerate the present and vilify the past does a disservice to both epochs. This book does neither. The story is appealing because it is well told within its own paradoxical coherent stream of consciousness and eidetic style. It is a meander into memories. It is personal and public. It is deceptively simple. Yet it tells of a time that did not know how rapidly change would overtake it, how imminent was its demise and how significant its influence on future generations would be.

Clinical Psychologist and author
MARIE MURRAY *is Director of Student Services in UCD and an* Irish Times *columnist.*

There is a place where our vanished days secretly gather
and the name of that place is memory ...
JOHN O'DONOHUE (1956–2008)

1 The House

I remember, I remember
The house where I was born ...

That's it there – second house on the right as you come in from the Mullingar Road. As I write, it is derelict – windows boarded up, holes in the roof, a 'For Auction' sign posted out front saying 'the site' is for sale. Inevitably it will be demolished and 'the site' will be filled with retail outlets and town houses. Imagine! Town houses in our garden ... now it is derelict – and it depresses me to see it so. But once it was solid, cosy, intimate. Once it was home – my home.

It is an unpretentious two-storey house, and small. Originally it had only two bedrooms until, following the death of Christy Fleming, the 'one-up, one-down' next door was annexed and we had a little more space. We did not own the house. My father rented it from a Mrs Meehan and every so often my father went to her house on the North Circular Road in Dublin to pay the rent. Imagine owning a house in Ballivor and not wanting to live there ...

Into the hall. To the right the 'good room' reserved for Christmas and special family occasions. The piano is there, where my siblings Kathleen, Mary and Noel literally suffered for their art under the strict tutelage of Miss Dunne who rapped their knuckles with a ruler when they got their scales wrong ... Maybe because of that, I was never put forward for piano lessons – something I now regret. The wind-up gramophone is there too – Mario Lanza singing 'The Loveliest Night of the Year' echoes in my memory. Do I hear Souza marches also? A lace tablecloth, the 'good' glasses (reserved for Christmas sherry), the beautiful oil-lamp. A fire was lit here on Christmas Day and my father would cry when he reflected on years past and departed family members.

Across the hall and into the kitchen. The hearth and heart of the home. The range is lit all year round, fuelled by turf hard-won from Coolronan bog – providing heat, cooking energy and hot water. In the evenings Kitty Carey will come up from the Post Office with her little canister for milk. She will sit before the range with my mother and Kattie Brown to exchange the news and gossip of the day. An occasional visitor is Hetty Dunwald – a beautiful post-war German refugee who worked in Master Conway's house. At the table I wrestle with my homework, under the stronger light of the 'tilly' lamp.

> *An old boot tells its story ... Parse and analyse the*
> *following sentence ... Find the cost of 5 tons, 3 cwts.,*
> *3 quarters of lime ...*

On the wall there are pictures of the Sacred Heart (with a tiny oil-lamp beneath) and Eoin O'Duffy, Commissioner of An Garda Síochána. There is a cupboard beneath the stairs. For weeks my brother Noel believed there was 'a pink horse' in that cupboard following a dream he had. For weeks I was wary of opening the door to it. There are few books in the house, which would not be unusual at the time. I remember a six-volume encyclopaedia – *Cassell's New Popular Educator* –which my father had bought for his own self-improvement.

Through the doorway and into the back kitchen, the work centre of the house where my mother will prepare food, will wash and scrub clothes, dishes, pots and pans – and children too. As a young boy I wanted to live forever with my mother in the back kitchen. Off the back kitchen is a storeroom. There is a mound of potatoes in the corner. Here I would secrete the four and ninepenny truck which I bought in Leddy's shop with stolen money ...

Acquiring the annex provided us with a sitting room and the luxury of a sofa, armchairs and an open fire. Overhead an extra bedroom, which enabled my mother to keep lodgers when Bord na Móna and the Electricity Supply Board came to town. Back to the front hall, up the squeaking bare stairs. On the left is my parents' room where I was conceived and born (I have a fragment of memory of lying in my cot beside their bed). To the right the children's room – L-shaped, with two beds, where we laughed and cried, slept and dreamed, fought and played. The girls would eventually move away to boarding school in Mountrath, Co. Laois, but I recall an occasion when we were all abed with mumps and to pass the time we composed a song about 'Gibney's (pub) – Clonard and Killyon'. Why we should choose to sing about a pub is a mystery but we had such fun in doing so.

Out the back is the yard – at first a tiny enclosed space – and beyond an open yard from where turkeys and hens wandered free into the long garden beyond. There is a turf shed backing up to the house, packed to the roof with winter fuel. Once I was the hero of the day, when I discovered a smouldering fire caused by a lighted cigarette butt dropped by a careless adult. Disaster averted. Down the yard there is a ramshackle wooden garage, and beyond, the pigsty where we kept a pig or two. And there's the privy – a little wooden cabin to which we traipsed in all weathers and in which we read the *Meath Chronicle* and the *Irish Press*, cut up into convenient squares by my father. The yard was also our playground where Noel and I contested hurling and football matches with such ferocity ... disputes, sulks, walk-offs ... and disaster when yet another ball was skied over the wall into Mrs Reynolds' yard. Goodnight Ballivor ... Mrs Reynolds *never* returned a ball.

It was small – barely adequate for our needs – unpretentious and modestly comfortable, but it was home. Secure, nurturing and warm. Our home. My home for the first fourteen years of my life.

2   The Girl from Tipperary

Bridget Ryan grew up near Killenaule in Co. Tipperary in a strong Catholic faith and was a daily Mass-goer all her life. It was therefore probably more than a quirk of fate that on her way into Mass on a morning in the early 1930s, she dipped her hand in the holy water font just as the tall, young garda sergeant dipped his. Hands touched, lives touched and a year or two later they married in Westland Row Church in Dublin, had their wedding breakfast in the Standard Hotel in Harcourt Street and probably a brief honeymoon in the city before beginning married life in the village of Pallaskenry in Co. Limerick, where the young sergeant was stationed. He was my father, Hugh Quinn, and Bridget Ryan was my mother, the girl from Tipperary, who was always proud of her Killenaule roots.

> *… I've lived in the valleys of fair Cashmere*
> *Under Himalay's snowy ridge;*
> *Then the other impatiently said 'See here,*
> *Were you ever at Laffan's Bridge?'*
>
> *… And I wouldn't care much for Sierra Leone*
> *If I hadn't seen Killenaule*
> *And the man that was never in Mullinahone*
> *Shouldn't say he had travelled at all …*
> 'THE TWO TRAVELLERS' – C.J. BOLAND

Bridget Ryan was one of eight children born to Patrick Ryan

and Mary Roche of Derricknew, Killenaule, Co. Tipperary. Patrick and Mary were in fact second cousins who met at a funeral. Patrick, my grandfather, worked on laying the Clonmel–Thurles railway line which ran by his house. Fifty years later his son Jack worked on removing the same track. I never knew my Tipperary grandparents and only came to know my uncles Mikey, Andy, Tom, Paddy and Jack and my aunt Ellie in their later years. Another aunt, May, died of tuberculosis in her thirties. It was only after my mother's death in 1984 that I first visited the house she was born and reared in. I had to go across the fields, through seven gateways and along the railway line to reach it.

On her deathbed, rambling through her childhood, my mother declared that the Ryans 'weren't rich, but we were honest and respectable ...' I am told that Granny Ryan would dress in her finery and travel in a pony and trap to Killenaule of a Saturday and proceed to Kennedys' snug for her glass of sherry. Rambling further, my mother confided in me that 'during the War of Independence Mikey Ryan told Jim Mockler that it was alright to steal a lamb to feed the lads in the hills ...'

Bridget, or 'Bridie', Ryan would only have had a primary education and would have worked at home before taking the train from Laffan's Bridge in search of employment as a shop assistant. A tall, fair-haired beauty, she loved to go dancing. Whenever the song 'Charmaine' came on the radio, it would trigger memories of the days she danced into the small hours of the morning. She loved life and she loved people. Her brother Mikey told me once how Bridie would go to Sunday Mass and invite a crowd back to their house for a dance that night.

'We'd know nothing about it until they all turned up that night. Fellows would come from as far away as Horse and Jockey with fiddles under their arms and we'd have a great night. One time when she was away working, she brought home a lovely gramophone with a pile of records – lovely *céilí* music and John McCormack songs. The best of stuff. 'Twas a wonder ... In the summertime we'd have dances too, down in the Ball Alley. In the wintertime we'd go down to Biddy Dwyer's house in the bog. Three or four of us would collect sixpence or a shilling from those present and we'd buy a quarter cask of stout for ten shillings, put it on the bog barrow and roll it down to Biddy's. The women would make tea and we'd have white bread and jam to eat and lots of dancing. That would do us for the week. We'd spend the rest of the week talking about it …'

When working in Athy, Bridie joined the local drama group and recalled playing opposite the well-known actor Denis O'Dea. She would not have wanted for suitors but that fateful dip of the hand in the holy water font put an end to all that.

In 1935 the young couple arrived in Ballivor, Co. Meath in their little Morris Cowley together with their firstborn, Kathleen. Over the next six years three more children would arrive – Mary, Noel and myself. My mother was a very positive person. She loved being with people and this – allied to her strong religious faith – gave her contentment and serenity. Whether it was an evening chatting by the fireside, a Sunday afternoon trip to Kellys' in the bog, or a visit to McGonagles' in Trim or Finucanes' in Dublin, she was happy being with friends. She did not ask much more from life.

Rearing a young family occupied most of her time but she also found the time and energy to raise turkeys, hens and pigs – out of necessity to supplement the family income. We were not the only children who were 'fed and clothed by pigs and turkeys'. Later, when Bord na Móna and the ESB came to the village, she would take in lodgers. My mother's cooking was legendary. She made her own bread, baked mouth-watering tarts and churned her own butter. Often when we came home from school we would be invited to 'take a turn at the churn'. It seemed to take forever turning the handle of the churn to spin it around until at last the little globules of butter appeared on top of the cream. Eventually my mother would shape them artistically with wooden butter pats until they sat glistening invitingly on the butter dish, waiting to be spread on the oven-fresh brown bread.

Life was tough for women in the post-war pre-electricity days. There were no modern conveniences such as a refrigerator, a cooker or a washing machine. There was the all-purpose range to provide cooking, hot water and heat. Then there were the washtub, the washboard for scrubbing and the wringer. The same washtub would be used to scrub the children of a Saturday night. As a small boy I, of course, idolised my mother! She was a happy person who would occasionally burst into song (I vaguely remember her playing the melodeon too) and to be with her was to be in a happy place. As my sister Mary picturesquely puts it – 'she had a great big heart and she would readily take it out and slice it for you'. Her love and care for her children were paramount and – like most mothers of her generation – she would put herself last and make whatever sacrifice was necessary for the wellbeing of her family. Her love also extended beyond the front door. She would send steak and kidney down to a neighbouring mother who was rearing a large family, to ensure that they got a nourishing stew regularly.

A day out would be a rarity for my mother. The Christmas outing to Dublin, a day at the seaside in Bettystown, a Sunday with her in-laws in Monaghan – these would be the highlights of her year. Or maybe a trip to Croke Park. I remember her accompanying my father and myself to my first All-Ireland Final – in 1953 when Kerry faced Armagh. Croke Park was packed (no tickets then – you just turned up at the turnstile!) – and huddled under the old Cusack Stand I panicked and began to cry, not for myself but for fear of my mother being hurt. She saw it differently and appealed to the steward to let us out on the sideline. Thankfully he did and scores of patrons were released. I was then able to watch the match in comfort from behind the goal and had a perfect view of Bill McCorry's missed penalty, which cost Armagh the match.

Once a year, or maybe less frequently, my mother would take off for a trip to her beloved Tipperary. All dressed up in her petrol-blue suit, her flowery hat and her fox fur, she would catch the train at the Hill of Down and by a circuitous route make her way to Laffan's Bridge in Tipperary, leaving my father in charge of us children. She would return a week later, full of stories from home and refreshed for the year ahead.

Above all else it was her faith and the consistent practice of it that energised my mother. All would be well and the Lord would provide. 'Thanks be to God we lived so long and did so little harm,' she would say. She died in 1984 and at her funeral her dear friend Mrs Finucane (mother of Marian) said to me – 'Do you know that your mother said fifteen decades of the rosary every day for you, her children?' I felt so grateful and inadequate, but not altogether surprised.

3   The Sergeant

He was a tall, well-built, upright man. Upright in his bearing, upright in his living. In 1935, he had come to Ballivor where for the next twenty years he would be known simply as 'the Sergeant'. He was my father.

Hugh Quinn was – as he proudly boasted – 'a '98 man'. He was born in 1898, one of seven children, on a small farm in Drumacon among 'the wee hills of Monaghan'. Being one of five boys growing up on that small holding during the troubled birth of a nation didn't offer many career prospects. He would have had a basic primary education, no more. There was a solid farming education too – he would recall being in charge of the ploughing at the age of fourteen. As he grew to manhood, however, it was evident that there was an abundance of manpower on the farm.

There was talk of passage money being sent back from an uncle in America, but then the emergence of the new state brought unforeseen employment opportunities. A new police force, *An Garda Síochána* (the Guardians of the Peace), came into being in 1922 and my father was one of the first to enrol. His official number was 2039. I can still see it imprinted everywhere – on official notepaper, on his uniform, on the inside of his cap. Following some rudimentary training in Kildare Barracks and initial postings in Mayo and Limerick, the young sergeant arrived with his wife and firstborn child into the quiet village of Ballivor in 1935.

The law was upheld by Sergeant Quinn
For whom unlighted bikes were the greatest sin.
The people's crimes kept his notebooks full
of uncut thistles and unlicensed bulls.
  Oh goodnight, Ballivor, I'll sleep in Trim.

For all its smallness and sleepiness, Ballivor and its environs had the luxury of being manned by a sergeant and four gardaí. The barracks was in effect a farmhouse with gardens and outhouses. Downstairs was a large dayroom with a big open fire, and an equally large unused room where my father stored a vast quantity of seed potatoes. At the back, the dreaded lock-up, where many a drunk slept off his 'abusive behaviour'. Upstairs provided garda accommodation. It was a strange, forbidding place for me. I never felt at ease there – it reeked of officialdom and authority. I was much more at home in its outhouses where my father pursued his other (and to my mind much more satisfying) career – farming.

Two milking cows and a couple of calves were housed in one building. Overhead, a hayloft where I hid and imagined strange worlds and epic deeds. A barn stocked with hay (and turf for the dayroom fire), pits full of mangolds and turnips – to be dug out on freezing winter evenings, scraped clean and run through the manual Pierce pulper. I see my father guide horse and plough through the garden areas on either side of the path that led to the barracks, checking, coaxing, urging the animal with a click of his tongue, a pull on the rein as he opens perfect drills for potatoes. I see myself helping him scatter manure along those drills and dropping those seed potatoes which had sprouted through the spring months in that dark and dank barrack room.

'Take it nice and cushy,' he says to me. 'Don't be carrying the lazy man's load' – when I overload a bucket with seed potatoes. When I snuffle with a runny nose, he stops and shows me how to clear it. Press your thumb on one nostril and blow hard on the other. 'Sure you're only throwing away what the gentleman puts in his pocket!' Uncontestable logic. I imagine he had learned that lesson from his father. He is thrifty, as the times dictate. Nothing is thrown away. A length of twine, an empty box, a nut and bolt. They will all 'come in useful' in time. 'You'll follow a crow for that some day,' he chides me for leaving an uneaten crust. He is meticulous in his work, taking it anything but 'cushy'. He sings a snatch of a song – 'South of the Border'. I know now that he dreams of a farm south of an Irish border, not a Mexican one. He is happy. I am happy.

Behind the barracks he cultivates a range of vegetables. Somewhere hidden among the onions and cabbages in the barrack garden is the rain-gauge, from which my father will take daily rainfall readings, note them (again meticulously) and forward them to some office in Dublin. My public father is the public servant, the Guardian of the Peace. 2039. The Sergeant. My private father is seated on a milking stool between two cows. I stand in the doorway listening to the music of the milking, the contented breathing and chewing of these placid animals in their stalls.

I have two fathers. The sergeant, serious and imperative in his uniform of brightly polished buttons and buckles. I admire him, fear him a little, fear for him in the execution of his duties. I am – as a local eccentric dubbed me – 'a limb of the law'. And there is Daddy, in working clothes, sleeves rolled up, driving a horse and hay bogey down the main street. In a little while he will return with an entire cock of hay, winched magically aboard the bogey. But now it is empty – until half the village children clamber aboard its spacious floor for a free ride through the village. Daddy – the Pied Piper. I love him.

4   '98 Man

For my father, on the centenary of his birth – 25 January 1998.

Born into a dying century
A primitive time
From our perspective
Few enough horizons
For a Monaghan ploughboy –
The emigrant ship, maybe
Or (thankfully)
A member of the newly-formed
Guardians of the Peace

    Upholder of the law
    Diligent in pursuit
    Of drunk and disorderly,
    Unlighted bikes
    And noxious weeds

Happier by far
Opening a furrow
Scattering dung
Or barrowing turf

    I hear you still
    Sing a snatch of

'South of the Border'
And tell me to
'Take it cushy'.

In your company
I was happier too
Unspoken contentment
In Johnny Kelly's bog
Or under the Cusack Stand.

Another century dies
In a world you would
Hardly recognise
Or tolerate

But on this January day
I feel your presence
And your absence too
Thank you, God bless you
And – take it cushy now ...

5 The Little Black Book

It is standard government issue – a small hard-backed notebook with the initials OAS (*Oifig an tSoláthair* – Office of Supplies) imprinted on its black cover. I came across it some years after my father's death in 1966. In that little black book 'the Sergeant' had officially noted the crimes, traumas, suspicions, trespasses, accidents, comings and goings of a whole community for the years 1939–1944. It is quite a remarkable social history of those war years. It is at this remove the stuff of both comedy and tragedy, of dark hidden worlds – worlds that I was totally sheltered from as a child – and of ways of life and death that are vanished and banished – thankfully, in most cases. Yet here in this little book are the diligently recorded minutiae of largely uneventful lives in a midlands village, interspersed with major tragedies and sorrows.

Had I the gift, I would love to paint a grand mural which would reflect the village life recorded in this book. That mural would be dominated by shadowy figures cycling down dusky roads on unlighted bikes. Page after page of the little black book lists the names of those lawbreakers who ventured into the night lightless and reflectorless well after lighting-up time (duly noted in each case). The mural would also depict roaming dogs. One 'swoop' on 29 February 1940 listed ten owners found in possession of fourteen unlicensed dogs. My mural would also depict the roads around Ballivor clogged with straying animals ...

Found five cows straying on road at Moyfeigher ...
Found six bullocks straying on road at Moattown ...
Found one donkey straying ... found one pony straying
... two goats straying at Portlester ... one bull straying on
the public road at Ballivor.

In some cases, poor fencing may have been to blame; in others the animals were deliberately left out to graze on the 'long acre' (the grass roadside verges) but people like Thomas McNamee had no excuse at all.

Found seven head of cattle straying on the public road at
Ballivor, property of Thos. McNamee, who left same go
away while he stopped in Walsh's licensed premises ...

A visit to a licensed premises would obviously render a man incapable of controlling animals.

At 7.30 p.m. found Christy McLaughlin drunk on the
roadside at Parkstown in charge of three cattle. The
handlebar of his bicycle was broken in two ...

Found John Ward drunk in charge of a horse and cart in
Kildalkey at 10 p.m. ...

You travelled the roads of Ballivor at your peril in the 1940s. And it seems the Gardaí, like the Mounties, always got their man ...

29.5.1941 Found Bernard Toner at 11 p.m. cycling
without a light. He refused to halt.
30.5.1941 Met B.T. cycling towards Kildalkey at
12.15 p.m.

Drink was undoubtedly the curse of the working man.

> *Found Frank Owens drunk in Ballivor and using filthy*
> *language ...*

Poor Frank! He would have been a regular feature in the little
black book. He would terrify me as he staggered up the street
roaring 'Up Drumlargan! *Sin é!*' And when the law descended
on a licensed premises after hours, those present had to think
on their feet – assuming they could stand on their feet ...

> *Inspected the licensed premises of P. Garry, Kildalkey, and*
> *found four men in the taproom with glasses of stout – Patrick*
> *and Thos. Harte, Patrick Kearney and Michael Hesnan. The*
> *Hartes stated they came in for cigarettes – and had a drink.*
> *Kearney came in for a dose for a horse – and had a drink.*
> *Hesnan came in for tobacco – and had a drink ...*

An entry for 13 June 1942 intrigues me.

> *Found Richard Harnan, Trim, and John Hennessy, no fixed*
> *abode, drunk in Ballivor. Both brought to barracks ...*

The question is prompted: was it either or both of those
gentlemen who first coined the phrase – *Goodnight Ballivor, I'll*
sleep in Trim ?
   Many of these entries mirror or presage scenes from the Wild
West movies that would later hold us in thrall.

> *24.9.1941 L.J.L. arrived home in Ballivor via train at*
> *Hill of Down.*

That terse entry might well come from the script of *High Noon*.
Then there was the inevitable sharpshooter riding into town,
making life difficult for the noble sheriff and the honest saloon-
keeper.

> *John J. McLaughlin, passenger on 1.15 p.m. bus, Dublin to Longford, stated he was asked for one shilling for half a whiskey from Columb Kelly, Ballivor. Called Mr Kelly a blackguard and a pup – and me likewise – and threatened to report us ...*

And how is this for *A Fistful of Dollars*?

> *18.11.1942 J.C. reported that he was informed by N.V. that C.V. offered him (N.V.) ten shillings to take his (C's) life on this date ...*

The recordings in this little black book depict life that I as a child was almost totally sheltered from. Oh yes, I knew about those unlighted bikes and the unlicensed dogs and the big poster in the barracks warning about the control of noxious weeds (ragwort, thistle and dock), but there was life and death out there that I was never to know.

> *29.3.1944 Private Patrick G., forty-seven years old, suffering from nerves since last Thursday, found in lavatory with his throat cut at about 2 p.m. at Coolronan camp. Two pounds, twelve shillings and sixpence ha'penny found in his possession ...*

A one-page entry from 1942 details the ravaging of one family in the space of a weekend by a merciless disease –

> *James Patrick, aged two years, died Sunday 19 July. Michael Francis, aged 13 months, died Monday 20 July. He had become ill on Friday 17. Una, Oliver and Joseph removed to Navan Fever Hospital at 8 p.m. on 20 July. Dr O. stated the illness was infantile paralysis.*

Children suffered in other ways too.

5.8.1940 James B., 10 years, boarded out with Mrs L., reported that she beats him for not working and he wants to go back to the Home in Trim.

Cruelty was not confined to young people.

11.11.1941 Found eleven head of cattle, property of Thomas G., that had their horns cut off and were bleeding a lot. Joseph C. admitted performing the operation on the cattle. No anaesthetic was used. C. stated he would get a bag of potatoes for doing the job. Two of the cattle were left in the house with sulphur put on the cut horns to stop them bleeding. The yard, walls and outhouses were very much covered with blood. Also Messrs C. and M. ...

Hard times. Ironically – and disappointingly – this is the nearest entry to my own date of birth. I turn the page expectantly, hoping my entry into this cruel world might at least rate a cryptic footnote, but no. The next entry concerns itself with a motor accident in February 1942, when a heifer calf was killed by a lorry. As with all motor accidents, there are endless measurements of road-width, tyre-marks, height of hedge, width of grass verge, etc.

Well of course my birth would not be noted. This is an official notebook. And yet occasional personal notes creep in:

20.2.1941 Paid £2 to John Kelly for one lorryload of turf.
2.3.1941 Paid £3.19.9 to Ml. Deery, Carrickmacross for 58 lbs of bacon.
5.6.1941 Wet battery put in radio.
20.7.1941 New Raleigh cycle no. DB58652 purchased by Sgt Quinn @ £9.10.0.
6.3.1942 Car greased at 23,780 miles.
7.5.1943 Paid Richard Walsh £10 for six days' turfcutting.

Elsewhere another page lists 'fixed prices' for a range of groceries –

> *Flour – 21 shillings per cwt., Bread – 5d., Cocoa 1/6d. per lb., Tea 3/9d., Rice and Sago 7d. per lb., Barley 9d. per lb.*

The most disturbing entry of all is dated 9.9.1941. It leaps out of the page at me –

> *Sgt. H. Quinn 2039 admits the four charges preferred against him overleaf. The sergeant's previous record in the service has been taken into consideration in arriving at a decision …*

My father the criminal? And what was the decision arrived at? I will never know, but given the times and mores, I suspect my father was in danger of being cashiered for sprouting seed potatoes on the barrackroom floor. Others suggest his crime was the unpardonable one of driving to Monaghan in wartime, but I prefer the image of the guilty potatoes sprouting in that dank and dark barrackroom.

These were innocent times, dark times and (with hindsight) amusing times.

The very last entry in the little black book reminds me (again) of how hard these times were for many people –

> *Christina B. working for John H. 9 a.m. to 10.30 p.m. each day of the week, including Sunday. No half-day.*

And if Christina did wish to escape from Ballivor, the Little Black Book duly notes that the morning bus departs at 9.56 a.m., arriving in Dublin at 11.18 a.m., while the afternoon bus departs at 2.48 p.m., arriving in Dublin at 4.10 p.m.

6   The Street I: South Side

Now for a stroll down the Main Street (I know, I know – the farther it goes, the 'maner' it gets ...) Ours is the second house from the top 'on the Kinnegad side'.

At the top, on the corner, lives Mrs Reynolds. A private and pious woman. A widow who – to my memory – always wore black. She had once been a teacher. I was always a little in fear of her and never really knew her. All I know is that she must have had an amazing collection of footballs, hurling balls, sponge balls ... all OUR balls. Past the Sergeant's house and on to Collins'. Joe and Katie, quiet and gentle neighbours. Next is Dempseys'. A busy house this, with eleven children. Frank Dempsey is the local postman but he is also a blacksmith and has a little forge down at the back of the house.

Now we're passing the Catholic church – sharing spacious grounds with the parochial house. The original church is thought to have been built shortly after the Catholic Emancipation Act of 1829, at the request of Catholic landowners the Browne and Rickard families. Both church and parochial house were dominated for an amazing forty-two years by Fr Patrick Farrell, who came originally from Castletown-Geoghegan in Co. Westmeath. A tall austere man who came to Ballivor in 1908, you trembled if he singled you out in the churchyard or on the street. He would ask you to recite a prayer or answer a question from the Catechism and you got a serious reprimanding if you stumbled in your reply.

Next is Pat McGearty's house, once a courthouse. Fifty years later it became a house of teachers when M.J., Bridie, Bernie, Josie and Maureen joined the profession. M.J. became 'Mr Ballivor' – trainer of under-age teams, keeper of the records, at the heart of the village's development over a long lifetime. Sean became a priest and served God in Australia and Patsy became an accountant with Bord na Móna. More importantly, he became goalkeeper with Meath and proudly represented us 'between the sticks' when Meath annexed their second All-Ireland in 1954 (for me there was no celebration of Sam's return – I was coming to terms with boarding-school life in Ballyfin).

Next door is the house of John McGearty, brother of Pat. Both Pat and John were ex-R.I.C. men. John's house was originally the R.I.C. barracks and the scene of an attack during the War of Independence, when an R.I.C. constable was killed. It was burned down in 1922. 'Mrs John' was originally principal of the Girls' School before it was merged with the Boys' School and she then taught the junior end of Ballivor N.S. Outside John McGearty's is an important landmark – the village pump. Ah – the endless trips up and down to that pump with my brother – the full bucket-load shared between us on a hurley. *(That's not fair – you keep making it slide down my side … Did not … Did so …)* Another twenty trips and the barrel will be full. And be careful how you prime that pump when the water level is low – otherwise the handle goes flying down and you do yourself a serious injury.

Passing Ludlows' now. There's Willie, Joe and Katie waving to us, but come upstairs. Here living and working in a dark, single room is the tailor Peter Whitty. He makes and mends and ekes out a lonely existence surrounded by materials and the tools of his trade – sewing machine, scissors, the intriguing tailor's chalk, measuring tape, assorted needles and a multitude of spools of thread. He is an artistic man – somewhere in the village is a painting of his, *The Family Rosary*. As children we relished a visit to his sparsely furnished room – we would hopefully acquire some empty spools and cloth offcuts to play with – but I always sensed that Peter was a lonely man, locked away in this shabby room. Each Sunday after Mass he would send two children to collect cigarette butts outside the church gate. He just about made it into the local cemetery. He avoided the Pauper's Grave at the bottom of the cemetery to be buried just inside the front wall. When paths were built his grave disappeared until Fr Sean McGearty honoured his name with a plaque. The memory of him still haunts me.

Now we come to Jabok's shop. His name was L'Estrange – how he came to be known as Jabok is a mystery. I seem to remember the signboard over the shop as something like 'Les Boco Stores'. It is claimed that he was a jockey who won a big race on a horse called 'Les Boco'. But Mr L'Estrange was only ever known as Jabok. For me, his 'stores' meant penny toffees and liquorice pipes but I am told he dealt in ironmongery and hardware. You could even buy a bed there, but as long as Jabok had liquorice pipes I was happy. One Halloween a few of the village 'boys' tried a prank which involved switching Jabok's signboard with that of Leddy across the street. Having removed Leddy's board, they couldn't budge Jabok's. Leddy's sign was ditched, never to be found again.

John Walsh's Grocery and Bar. John is affectionately known as 'The Pope' – presumably because of the resemblance he bore to the pontiff Pius XI. Mrs Walsh was a teacher who taught in Ballivor before 'going on the panel' and having to teach in Boher, near Mullingar. She would cycle to Hill of Down railway station to catch a train to Mullingar. Her children May and Raymond followed her into the teaching profession. Next door is Katie Commons who cleaned and decorated the church. She wore her hair in plaits and she was one of the first people in the village to have a radio, so neighbours would be invited in to listen to Joe Linnane's *Question Time* or an important football match. Katie also rented out rooms to Janey McKeown the dressmaker and to Mr Ginnett the cobbler, who came on his bicycle from Raharney. In this way the village was self-contained – tailor, dressmaker, cobbler, butchers, general stores, drapery, public houses. All material needs could be satisfied.

We move on to McKeowns' and say hello to Joe, Jamesy, Andy, Mick and Bridie – who would marry blacksmith Bill Kelly. Dargans is next door. Peter Dargan the farmer and butcher and his wife the teacher in Coolronan school (so many teachers in one street!). Before she sets out on her bicycle she will call out to the yardman, 'Finglas, go out and see what way the wind is blowing!' They have seven children, of whom Rita will become a doctor and Dinah (another) teacher, Peter Junior will become a veterinary surgeon and head of the Irish Veterinary Union, while Michael J. will become one of the village's best-known sons – rising to the very top in Aer Lingus. Next is Hineys' where there are six more children. Large families are a feature of the street – eleven Dempseys, nine Browns, eight McGeartys, seven Dargans, five Kellys, five McLaughlins. While they would not all be contemporaneous, a rough tally indicates that there would have been up to eighty children or young people living in the village at that time (today, I am told, there are six). Mrs Hiney, as the local midwife, delivered and weighed in most of the children in the village and kept mothers informed on the latest family developments.

There is a gap now until the next building, but down the alleyway are two contrasting businesses. On one side the sounds and the smells of Bill Kelly's forge (see *The Forge*) and on the other the silent and dark world of mushrooms, grown by Mr Musial – an early Polish immigrant. The last shop in the village is Geoghegans' – or Murtaghs', as it became known when the widow Nancy Geoghegan married John Murtagh. It is a grocery shop with a butchery – or victualler's shop, as it was grandly known – attached, run by Matt Peppard. It was to Geoghegans' I would repair on a Sunday morning after Mass, guiltily clutching the few sixpences and threepenny bits I had filched from the church offering plate ... There is surely no hope for me. I am damned for all eternity – but nevertheless I order a glass of lemonade and a sixpenny ice-cream ... let the ice-cream sink into the lemonade and it looks just like what they have in those American soda fountains in the pictures. Cool or what?

Mrs Geoghegan's house next door was a card-playing house to which my father, Harry Garry and others would go for serious games of Twenty-Five of a Sunday evening. Another gap now to Owen Gallagher's tidy little house and then on to Bob and Mary Sherrock's fine two-storey house. They have three sons – Bob, Jack and Mick – and a thriving haulage business, but most of all they own a large garage which on winter Sunday nights became for us the palace of dreams, the theatre of non-stop action ... (see *Cinema Paradiso*)

Over the little bridge that crosses the stream where we fished for pinkeens each summer, and up the hill to the last house on this side of the Trim Road – the Glebe – wherein lived the Protestant rector, Mr Thompson. The house was obscured from the road, surrounded by trees and approached via a winding avenue. It would be out of bounds to most of us. I cannot recall ever seeing the actual house. Mr Thompson's son, Eric, brought further honour to the village when he became Master of the Rotunda Maternity Hospital in Dublin.

7   Cinema Paradiso

Sherrock's Garage was a solidly unremarkable building on the Trim Road at the end of the village. A little stream ran by it and there I spent summer hours catching pinkeens (minnows) in a jam jar. The garage was functional in servicing the cattle trucks that formed Bob Sherrock's haulage business. It was spare and draughty. An oil-stained work bench ran down one side; a couple of tyres and a few oil drums were piled against the back wall. Oil-soaked sawdust covered the floor. A distinctly unwelcoming place – but on successive Sunday nights during the winter Sherrock's Garage was transformed into our Cinema Paradiso.

The transformation was rudimentary. A giant sheet draped over the inside of the entrance door. Rows of wooden benches, some tiered seating and a liberal scattering of sawdust. Still cold and draughty and reeking of oil and grease. But when Siki Dunne arrived from Kinnegad with his projector and three silver boxes containing the cine-reels of his 'one night only' presentation, we – his willing customers – were the ones who were transformed into cops, gangsters, cowboys, Indians, heroes and villains, as we were simultaneously transported to teeming cities, seedy nightclubs, stark prisons and lonely deserts. Many years later I wrote a poem about this experience. It was the first piece of writing that I had published – in the *Sunday Press*.

For One Night Only

Siki Dunne set up a picture show
Each Sunday night in Sherrock's Garage.
'Next Attraction –
James Cagney in White Heat –
For one night only –
Full supporting programme.
Eight-thirty p.m. SHARP!'
(In other words, no dawdling after devotions, folks).
Dawdle?
We shed our surplices and candle-greased soutanes
With unholy zest
And scuttled down the street
Lured by the siren strains of Rosemary Clooney's
Comeonamyhouseamyayhouse
Deserting God for a shilling dose of Mammon.

And there
Careless of grease-pocked wooden seats
Oil-soaked sawdust and icy draughts
We surrendered to the celluloid world
And warmed in the glow
Of Cagney's White Heat.

Later
We fought a famous gun-battle in the shadowy street,
Dropped into 'Sam's' for a bourbon with ice,
Slapped Micky Fagan behind bars
And raced off home as he whined
'You guys! You guys can't pin this rap on ME!'

Next morning in the frosty light
There was no Plaza or Savoy,
but Sherrock's Garage
And Manhattan Sam – the village pump –

Stood stiffly in his regulation
County Council coat of straw.
Someone had sprung Micky Fagan too –
The hoary church gates lay open
As we trooped back to serve
Our other master.
(Mass begins at seven-thirty SHARP,
said Father Farrell.)
But Jimmy Cagney had blazed into our lives
For one night only.

Cagney was but one of our tough-guy heroes. We spoke out of the corners of our mouths like Bogart, rode tall in the saddle like Randolph Scott and tried desperately to raise our eyebrows like Robert Mitchum. We called each other *no-good hoodlums* and *ornery sidewinders*, headed the redskins off at the gulch and stomped off home in a sulk when the two-bit bank robber refused to acknowledge that he had been plugged between the eyes during the heist. There were films with strange titles like *Johnny Belinda*, *Key Largo* and *Hungry Hill*. We devoured them all.

Occasionally a travelling 'fit-up' cinema came our way. I remember one that set up in Commons' field and enthralled us for a week with the terrifying serial *The Clutching Hand*. It would be a brave lad who would walk home on his own after that experience. There was also a feature film – *The Four Feathers* – which told tales of cowardice and bravery in Sudan when the sun still shone on the Empire.

The rain might have leaked through the canvas roof and our legs might have dangled in foot-high grass but still we baked on the plains of India and suffered unspeakable torture. When the fit-up moved on we searched in the long grass for film off-cuts – censored bits or the result of clumsy attempts to fix a broken reel – and held them up to the light, hoping they would reveal a swordfight and not a soppy kiss.

8 The Street II: North Side

Come along the Trim road for about a half-mile until you reach a part of the wall of Parkstown Estate that was (once) white. You will be following in the footsteps of the many who used stroll out to the 'White Walls' on a Sunday afternoon for recreation – just to sit there, tarry awhile, watch the meagre traffic go by and exchange the latest gossip ... We'll tarry not now, for in truth the traffic is very busy, there isn't much of a roadside margin and the walls are no longer white. But take a look across the field at the impressive Parkstown House – an imposing three-storey building which in my childhood was the home of the McKay family. John and Desmond went to Ballyfin boarding school, like ourselves the Quinns (often a tradition grows up in these matters within a village – the Dargans had also gone to Ballyfin). There are also twin McKay girls – Agnes and Eileen. We turn back to the village now, passing the tiny house that was home to the Cummins family. This house was obviously originally a gate lodge to Parkstown House. I spent many happy hours in this little house as John Joe and Willie Cummins were playpals of mine.

Back down the little hill and into the village where during my childhood McEvoy's Garage was built. I recall playing hide and seek with my pals in and out through the skeletal building. One of the builders asked us if we were playing 'conukio' and of course we called him by that name henceforth. The point was that we weren't seen as a nuisance or as a health and safety risk. We were welcomed. Adults had time for us. In January 1950, before the building opened officially, a charity dance was held in McEvoy's Garage. I hope 'Conukio' had a good night. Indeed, that night there was a problem – how to make the floor 'slippery' for the waltzers and the quick-steppers. One bright spark suggested sprinkling paraffin oil liberally on the floor (health and safety had not entered the lexicon then!). Come the night of the grand dance and a grand crowd turned up to trip the night away. Unfortunately the grand crowd generated a lot of body heat and this, combined with oil (more paraffin) heaters, caused paraffin fumes to rise from the floor … I'm sure the local belles were only too happy to 'step outside for a lemonade and custard cream'. Thankfully, nobody lit a match!

'Nobber Agin the Globe!' was the wonderful catch-cry of Jim Crosby who lived with his brother Tom in the next house on the village street. The brothers had obviously originated in the North Meath village. Jim would later marry the dressmaker Katie McKeon. Her niece, Greta Monahan, lived with the Crosbys. Next door are Mick and Mary Conlon. Now we come to another crowded house – Browns' – where there are nine siblings – Jim, Jack, Tony, Joe and five attractive sisters – Mary, Kattie, Nola, Lily and Maggie. Part of their house is let to Michael and Angela Leddy, who keep a drapery shop with occasional toys. The latter were my downfall when I succumbed to temptation on seeing a truck priced at four and ninepence in the window. Again, illicitly obtained church money funded the operation. To make matters worse, I get little satisfaction from my purchase as I must keep it hidden under the potatoes at home, because I cannot explain how I afforded it … Mr Leddy is very much the village eccentric, who will hold a hanky before his face at Mass if he does not wish to look at someone, and will busily de-wax his ears with same hanky during Fr Farrell's sermon. He refers to me as 'a limb of the law'. If anyone enters the shop he will peer out from the living room and call, 'There's something in the shop, Angela'. I am told he worked originally as a railway station master in England and only became eccentric when shares plummeted in value on the outbreak of war.

At Christmas 1944 Hugh Gunn opened his chemist's shop next door to Browns' and over the following decades he ministered to all our ailments. The shop was built on the site of Nixon's Garage, where concerts and variety shows had been performed. Lizzie Nixon ran the post office next door, with the assistance of people like Della Mannion and Kitty Carey, not forgetting Lizzie's faithful dog, Tim. For years the post office housed the only public telephone in the village and so was the source of the first news of births and deaths. The telegram was a vital service provided by the post office and was equally a vital source of income for a young boy like myself who could earn sixpence or a shilling (depending on distance) delivering good news and bad on his mother's bicycle. The Ballivor telephone directory in the 1950s was not very extensive. Ballivor 1 was the post office. Ballivor 2 – the Garda station. Ballivor 3 – Bord na Móna. Ballivor 4 – parochial house. Ballivor 5 – Barney Eivers (vet). Ballivor 6 – Charlie Flattery (auctioneer). The post office was also a source of delight on the occasions when postman Frank Dempsey would deliver a great roll of newspaper 'funnies' sent to us by Uncle Paddy in the USA. Although we were culturally divided from them, we nonetheless devoured the adventures of Li'l Abner, Charlie Brown, Blondie and Dagwood and many more, most of them *in colour*.

The Greyhound Bar was owned by Columb and Frances Kelly, who had five children – Joe, Tom, Mary, Hilary and Pat. I played a lot in Kellys' – whether endlessly belting a ball against the broad gable end, or watching the intriguing process of bottling and labelling stout in the bottling store. The Kellys had class. They employed a maid, a housekeeper and two 'yardmen'. They kept greyhounds. And it was said that Mrs Kelly had a roomful of shoes! They had a wind charger in the garden (early eco-pioneers). And they had a summer house in the garden – an unheard-of luxury. Here we children would put on our own variety shows. I can still hear Joe Brown's lovely soprano voice ringing out on a summer evening –

> *It's a corner of Heaven itself*
> *Though it's only a tumbledown nest*
> *But with love brooding there*
> *Why no place can compare*
> *With my little grey home in the west …*

Let's go a little way up the Kildalkey road, turning right at the Greyhound Bar. On the right is the Protestant school, defunct in the fifties and now home to the Maye family. Tommy Maye had come from Dublin as a Bord na Móna electrician. I became friendly with his son Camillus and the large schoolroom became our playroom on many wet afternoons. Across the road is McQuaids'. Mr McQuaid was the Protestant dean who in his latter years was wheeled out in his bath-chair by his daughter Mary. The big attraction of McQuaids for us was their beautiful orchard which we regularly targeted for raids – whenever Mrs McQuaid was not sitting out under an apple tree. It later became the home of Charlie and Mary Flattery. They had the luxury of a pump in the yard. This I know because my father rented grazing in the field across the road and I would have to draw water from that pump and pour it down a chute into a barrel in the field. I seem to have spent a lot of my childhood drawing water. Maureen McGearty even remembers me arriving at the village pump on my tricycle with a bucket on the handlebars.

Before we return to the village, a quick step up the road to the 'new' cemetery (as opposed to the old cemetery in Kilaconnigan). The story of any village is told in its burial grounds. These are lines I wrote in this cemetery in 2001 –

> *Eighth of December*
> *(when my mother would bring*
> *the turkeys to Dublin …)*

I stand in a mild winter sun
And relive my childhood.
As I wander through these gravestones
the names come swimming back –
Joe and Katie Collins
our next-door neighbours;
Master Conway –
'When I was in Marseilles ...'
– his wife and their triplets
who lived but weeks ...
Terry Connor and Berna Dempsey
my school pals;
Barney Eivers the vet
who courted my sister
and brought me with him
to treat strange ailments
like timbertongue and red murrain;
Peter Whitty the tailor
who lived in one room –
I remember his marking chalk;
Foxy Ryan and the Pope Walsh.
And there are my godparents
Bill Davis and Nan Miggin;
Jimmy Murray
the ballad voice of Ballivor –
just a few weeks here.
God rest and thank you all,
for I am part of you
and you are part of me.

Back to the village and across the Kildalkey road from the Greyhound Bar is the Protestant church, St Kinneth's – standing directly opposite the Catholic church of St Columbanus. It was built in 1821 on a site given by the landlord, Lord Darnley. Lady Darnley donated the silver plate. It was forbidden ground for us children – I never saw the interior of St Kinneth's until

1997. The grounds were a jumble of graves and undergrowth, dominated by huge beech trees which resounded each evening with the cacophony of roosting crows. When those trees shed their leaves in the autumn, the village girls (and maybe a boy or two!) gathered them into mounds on the footpath and built leaf houses – which the naughty village boys would eventually demolish. Entering the grounds – never mind the church – was forbidden, but that did not stop Johnny Dempsey scaring us all one Halloween when he appeared on the church wall dressed in a sheet. I even crept in there myself on another Halloween when I tied thread to Joe Collins' door knocker, ran the spool across the road and into the Protestant church grounds. Of course the first car that came down the street ruined all my plans.

Guard Maguire and family lived next door to the Protestant church. Later, bus driver Jim Brown and his wife Isabella would move in there. Next was the butcher's shop, originally with Jimmy and Tony Heavey and later with the Whelehans – Kevin and Jimmy from Killucan. In between serving customers, their assistant Sean Egerton would play football across the street with us, even though it was an unfair contest. His 'goals' were the shop door, three feet wide, while we had to defend a twelve-foot gateway. And finally to Joe McLaughlin's General Stores – Bar, Lounge, Grocery, Hardware and Drapery. Joe and Bella McLaughlin had five children – Philo, Maura, Breda, Catherine and Robert – but their emporium and the services it provided deserve a chapter of their own (see *General Stores*).

9 The Street III: Around the Corner

Jack McLough (an abbreviation of McLoughlin) worked in Joe McLoughlin's farmyard. He lived out the Mullingar Road so we will complete our tour of the village starting at Jack's house and moving back towards the village. Next door is Harry Hamilton's house with the garage which has an intriguing horseshoe-shaped door. Now we are passing the teacher's residence where Master Conway and his wife and their eight children live – right next door to the school. On the other side of the school is Dixons', home of our 1949 hero Paddy 'Stonewall' Dixon, whose greatest fan was undoubtedly his mother. She could be heard in Croke Park bellowing 'Come on our Paudgeen!'

The field next to Dixons' was the venue for various 'fit-up' and travelling shows. I remember coming home from school and being serenaded by a blonde showgirl singing –

When you're smiling, keep on smiling
And the whole world smiles with you.

Easy for her – she didn't have to worry about the *Aimsir Fháistineach* or the cost of wallpapering a room. Further in is the football field – our very own field of dreams – although in truth few enough dreams were realised there.

Davis's shop is down in a hollow on the corner. Bill and Betty Davis have three children – Eileen, Lou and Tony – and

Bill is my godfather, which is good enough for an occasional toffee bar. Not far to go now. Out the Kinnegad road and first on the right is the Garda barracks, whose gardens I know so well. The barracks was once the parochial house – gifted to Fr Shaw, first parish priest of Ballivor, by the Robinson family. In the early 1950s the site between the barracks and the Ballivor river (well, it was a river to us!) was developed when the County Council built a terrace of semi-detached houses. Among those who moved in were the Dempsey and Cummins families and Bill Kelly the blacksmith – who promptly named the development 'the Burma Road' after recent wartime events (Bill would also name the later Bord na Móna development on the Mullingar Road as 'Red Square' ...) Across from Burma Road there is one house – that of hackney-driver Mickey Miggin. Mickey and Nan Miggin have two children – Doreen and Seamus – who become playmates of mine. Nan, kindly Nan, is my fairy godmother (my real godmother was her sister-in-law, Tess) so there are regular baking treats on offer. There is a lot to be said for living within fifty yards of both your godparents.

Home now, round by Mrs Reynolds' corner. I must inspect the wall closely to see if there is any reminder of the day I careered into it on my bicycle. Having practised riding the bicycle in the football field, I ventured out on the public road, panicked at the sight of the first car and smashed painfully into Mrs Reynolds' wall. It was all part of a Ballivor education.

10 General Stores

In Joe McLaughlin's General Stores
– or, as the signboard said, General Joe McLaughlin
Stores –
They sold Indian meal and women's drawers
Rat traps, rashers and six-inch nails,
Pints of porter, stout and ales.
O goodnight Ballivor, I'll sleep in Trim.

'General' Joe McLaughlin came from 'Tyrone among the bushes' (as he would style it) to County Meath, married Isabella, or 'Bella', Garry and opened his General Stores in Ballivor – across the street from our house – in 1933. In the days before supermarkets, the General Stores met practically all the basic needs of a community, combining grocery, drapery and hardware supplies with a public house. But it was more than the sum of all those parts. It was a true community centre, a meeting place which provided many social services – some official, some unofficial. Joe's daughter, Breda, worked in the drapery shop, having served her time in Arnotts in Dublin, and I am indebted to her for an insight into the General Stores.

When Joe married Bella he not only acquired a beautiful wife, he also acquired a brother-in-law – Harry Garry – who spent his working life serving in the shop. Always cheery, greeting young and old with a smile and a ready quip, Harry was much loved by all. He remained a bachelor all his life and lived for the late-night card games in Geoghegans', from which he would return whistling his way up the dark street (in reality, Harry wasn't the bravest of souls!). He would then climb in through the dining-room window and make his way to bed.

If I was lucky enough to acquire a 'tanner' (a sixpenny-piece) I would go straight over to Harry to exchange it for six pennies in the innocent belief that I now had more money. Harry would play along with the idea and convince me that I was now a man of substance ... To be of real substance, you might have a 'bob' (shilling), a 'florin' (two shillings) or a 'half-dollar' (half-crown). (I never had a crown until I gave one to my wife during our wedding ceremony as a 'token of my worldly goods'.) I marvelled at how deftly Harry could tie up a parcel, loop the twine around his fingers and break it with a sharp tug. Anytime I tried that particular trick I failed – and went close to amputating several fingers.

Parcelling and tying were very much a part of a shop assistant's day. There was fine paper for the initial wrapping and strong paper for the final wrap. The assistant would also be expected to tie the parcel to the customer's bicycle. The range of grocery goods was quite limited and much of it came in bulk, so shop assistants spent a lot of their time weighing and packing goods like tea, sugar, flour, dried fruit. Joe McLaughlin was horrified one day to see a shop assistant shake some sugar from a two-pound bag back into the sack. 'Sure, that's your profit,' the assistant laughed. True to his Northern tradition of being straight and honest, Joe berated his assistant. The weights from all the shops in the village were subject to scrutiny at regular intervals by the Weights and Measures Inspector who operated in the courtroom in Pat McGearty's house.

We think of recycling as a modern phenomenon but fifty or sixty years ago it was practised perforce, as materials were scarce. A tea chest could become a play pen or a trailer for a bicycle; surplus twine would be rolled into a ball for re-use; a strong butter-box could serve a multitude of uses in the home. The grocery/hardware shop was quite small and was dominated by large bins of Indian meal, flour and clarenda (a kind of chicken food), but whether you wanted a loaf of bread (from Kellys of Kilcock), six-inch nails or leather for shoe repairs (sold by weight), Harry Garry was your man. Beyond the grocery were the bar and snug. A lounge bar was a fifties phenomenon. I recall having my Confirmation photograph taken in 1954 in the newly opened McLaughlin's Lounge Bar ('... and, for goodness' sake, take that orange out of your jacket pocket').

At the other end of the general stores was the drapery shop – run for years by Julia Smith – where you could buy anything from net curtains ('they're the same length as a newspaper page') to a funeral habit (brown only). Breda recalls Christmas as being a particular challenge. 'You had to think for your customers, know what they could afford and find something from a limited range – hankies, teacloths, oilcloths for the table, stockings and fur-lined gloves (a favourite for girlfriends).' The drapery shop was an important meeting place for older people particularly, although it was also a custom for mothers to send a child up to the shop with notes ('please give Mary a white man's hanky ...'!). The hours were long in the grocery and drapery. They were open until ten o'clock p.m., and on Saturday night men came up to the drapery shop from the bar at that time – and expected to be served.

McLaughlin's General Stores went far beyond being a shop. It was a depot for Prescotts' Dry Cleaners. On Fair Day McLaughlin's house was a bank depot (on one memorable fair day, a bullock tried to make a deposit by charging in through the front door). It provided a notice board for advertisements ('Cot for sale with inferior sprung mattress'). And on a personal service level, Breda was prevailed on to write letters for customers ...

Breda: *And what will I say?*
Customer: *Just tell them we are well and hope to see them soon.*

Breda: *And how will I close it?*
Customer: *Just put 'Yours in Jesus Christ' ...*

The third generation of McLaughlins continues to serve Ballivor in the twenty-first century. The notion of a general stores has long gone but there is a generation which fondly remembers Harry Garry weigh a half-stone of clarenda with a joke and a laugh. And there is a boy who remembers Harry trading six whole pennies for a sixpenny piece and giving him a knowing wink to confirm that he had done the right thing.

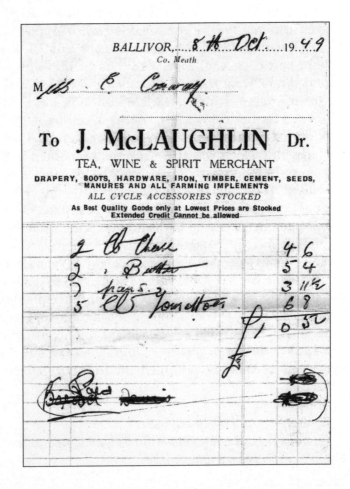

11 Radio Days

I waited anxiously for the little red light to come on. It took time to 'warm up'. The wireless. We never knew it as a radio – that elegant Pye receiver sitting on its own shelf in the kitchen. As I waited, my eye strayed across the station names on its panel – Hilversum, Warsaw, Munich, Brussels, Moscow, Athlone ... At last the machine came to life and I was transported into other worlds, from Gaelic games via Micheál O'Hehir to the daring adventures of Dick Barton, Special Agent.

For as long as I can remember there was a wireless in our house. In the 1940s not every house could boast such a luxury and it was not unusual for people to crowd into our kitchen or that of Katie Commons down the street to hear 'the match', or *Question Time* on a Sunday evening. Whenever there was a big match coming it was essential to be forewarned and have the 'wet battery' charged in Mick Smyth's garage in Trim. The worst possible scenario was to hear O'Hehir in full flight –

> '... *he bends, he lifts, he strikes. Tony Reddan in the Tipp goal throws himself full length* ...'

And then nothing.

> *Ah the feckin' battery's gone! Run down to Katie Commons' and see if he scored* ...

The news, of course, dominated the day and would be listened to without fail, even if – as often was the case – it barely changed throughout the day. There were stories of bad communists imprisoning Cardinal Mindszenty, of Panmunjon and the 39th Parallel in Korea, of a crisis in Suez. I hoped all those wars and troubles would never come near Ballivor. As I left for school, I was reassured by my father singing along with the signature tune of *Housewives' Choice* on the BBC Light Programme. *Doodle-um-a-doodle-um-a doodle-um*, he sang. All was well with the world.

We listened to the BBC because Radio Éireann 'closed down' for parts of the day. Thus I became familiar with *Music While You Work, Workers' Playtime*, even *Mrs Dale's Diary*. There was the fascination with the formally intoned shipping forecast:

> *'Shannon, Irish Sea, Fastnet, Lundy, Sole. Fresh or strong south to south-west winds. Occasional rain or drizzle. Visibility becoming moderate or poor, with some fog banks. Plymouth, Portland, Wight, Dover, Thames, Humber ...'*

Victor Sylvester and his strict-tempo orchestra played requests for 'Rita Banderchuk in Ceylon and Mark and Felicity Hamilton-Brown in Papua New Guinea'.

The wireless was my world. I developed a fascination for Max Robertson's wonderful tennis commentaries from Wimbledon.

> *'... Hoad, deep on the baseline, hoists a tremendous lob. Rosewall scurries back to retrieve it, takes it on the forehand; half-volley by Hoad, advancing to the net. Rosewall whips a forehand cross-court, passes Hoad, just out ...'*

Ken Rosewall became my hero, but he would never win Wimbledon.

Occasionally there was the thrill of getting up in the middle of the night to listen to a boxing commentary from across the Atlantic.

> *'And now we cross to Madison Square Garden in New York for commentary on the heavyweight title fight between Rocky Marciano and Jersey Joe Walcott. Commentary is by Raymond Glendenning with inter-round summaries by Barrington Dalby ...'*

Of all the delights the BBC had to offer, nothing compared with the adventures of Dick Barton, Special Agent. The 'Devil's Gallop' music stole me away at 6.45 each evening as I accompanied Dick and his pals Jock and Snowy on the most dangerous of missions. We rescued the lovely Laura and thwarted the evil Dr Kramer who had a plan to blow up all of London, but it was relentless and a special agent's work was never done. As we pursued the mad Kramer in a high-speed car chase, we worried if Jock would get to Kramer's house in time to release Snowy before the deadly gas was released. And then – a last throw of the dice by Kramer forces us off the road and we are hurtling helplessly into the ravine below ...

> *'Will Dick regain control of the car? Has Kramer escaped? And what of Snowy? Will Jock be in time to save him? Tune in tomorrow night for more adventures of – DICK BARTON, SPECIAL AGENT'*

How on earth could I concentrate on my homework after that? *Find the cost of 7 cwt., 3 qrs and 36 lbs of oats @ £2/1/8d. a cwt.* ... For God's sake, Master Conway, Dick Barton is *hurtling* towards his *death* – and you want me to think about *oats*!

There was, of course, drama on Radio Éireann but of a more sedate kind. Coming home for dinner each day from school (lunch had not yet been invented) enabled me to keep up to date with *The Kennedys of Castleross*. There was drama too for the much put-upon Tom Foley of *The Foley Family*. Little did I then think that a quarter of a century later I would enter a career in radio. 'Alice Foley' (Pegg Monahan) would become a dear friend, but the greatest surprise of all was meeting 'Tom Foley' (George Greene). I had always seen him as a big, brash, barrel-chested Dub, but George Greene was a wizened little man, crippled by arthritis. The power of radio. The power of the voice.

The richest drama of all came via Micheál O'Hehir from the Gaelic games playing fields. Even the most mundane games fizzed with passion and excitement through O'Hehir's repertory of cliché –

> *'there's a bit of a schemozzle in the square ...*
> *time is tick-tick-ticking away ...*
> *he bends, he lifts, he strikes ...*
> *what this game needs now is a goal ...'*

The commentary was interspersed with intriguingly anonymous messages ...

> *'From Glengariff Parade within hail of Croke Park come greetings to two boys who hope to journey from Chicago to New York, just to hear the game ... just as the family in Balla, Co. Mayo sends greetings to East 206th Street, New York ...'*

Radio accompanied me through the day. I prayed that sleep would come before the *Hospitals' Sweepstakes* programme wafted up to my bedroom from the kitchen below, because the rich, solemn tones of Ian Priestly Mitchell's voice – *when you wish upon a star* – always made me cry. But sleep would come and in the morning I would set off for school, comforted by my father's voice – *doodle-um-a-doodle-um-a-doodle-um*. All would be well with the world. Dick Barton would probably grab that overhead branch as his open-topped car *hurtled* to oblivion ... *Doodle-um-a-doodle-um*. All would be well.

12 Low Babies

On 7 May 1945, the German army surrendered to the Allied Forces. World War II was over. Seven months later I went to school for the first time, having reached the age of four. There is no connection between the two events. I have no memory of either, but suffice it to say they each played a major role in my life.

The school I attended was basic in its design and similar to hundreds of other rural schools of the period (it was built in 1864). A cut-stone building comprising a porch and two large rooms, each with an open fire. A roughly gravelled playground with a turf shed in the corner, and at the back, boys' and girls' toilets, which were so fetid and unhygienic that you did your best to stay clear of them, hoping you could last out until you got home.

Mrs John McGearty taught the junior end of the school – low babies, high babies, first and second class. She was severe in manner – she badgered us for tables and tidiness as we made our first attempts at writing on the *cláirín* – the slate, a relic of the Victorian era. Later we would graduate to copybooks, pens with nibs that you hoped would not strain and ink that you hoped would not blot. We practised proverbs in our Vere Foster copybooks –

> *All that glistens is not gold.*
> *Time and tide wait for no man.*

I bit my lip as I endeavoured to keep my writing between the blue lines and hoped above all that I would avoid the ultimate crime – a blot on my copybook. That would surely incur the wrath of the teacher and a penalty of either a verbal withering or a slap or two, which only added to the trembling in the fingers when I made a fresh attempt to get the line right.

There were more pleasurable moments, of course – playing with *márla* or plasticine and making patterns with seeds. We chanted our prayers and our tables aloud and listened while Mrs McGearty read a story to us – one of *Aesop's Fables* maybe, or a poem. I recall one about 'A Boy's Pocket', following which she asked me to empty my own pockets, and I was utterly embarrassed when the contents almost matched those of the boy in the poem.

She introduced us to the notion of sin (i.e. *real* sin, as opposed to blotting your copybook) as she prepared us for First Confession and First Communion. We racked our little brains for ways in which we might have offended the Almighty. She taught us hymns and songs. No doubt she was thorough and earnest – but she could be very cross! When I saw her death notice in the paper in 1973 I wrote these lines. Not great poetry, but a humble attempt to encapsulate her part in my life –

> *McGearty, at her son's residence,*
> *Middlesex, England*
> *Margaret, N.T.,*
> *Widow of the late John McGearty ...*
>
> * * *
>
> *The feel of plasticine*
> *Stand round the wall for your English reading*
> *The clammy dampness*
> *At the bottom of the room*
> *The smell of heaped-up oilskins drying out*
> *Someone did it in his pants*
> *– Hold your nose –*
> *Ceadagamdulamach?*

She sat above, back to the fire
And peered over her glasses
A pleasanter smell
Of turf-mould and ash up there,
And boy, could she be cross!
Indeed, she badgered you
For blots on your copybook.
Listen to the scraping of strained nibs
As she sits above in judgement
And calls forth the accused
To answer the charges ...

I remember trembling one day
When she summoned me
To empty my pockets
On her table.
I trembled
Because mine had all the things
A boy's pocket should have –
A nail, string, marbles
And a penny.
But I feared the laughter
When she would be proved right ...

God rest you, now –
To me you never grew older
Even when much later
I followed your path.
I always remembered you
As you were, when I was
In Low Babies and prayed
I wouldn't do it in my pants ...

And now you rest
In Middlesex soil.
Would you not be more at home
In Kilaconnigan?

13 The Master

Master Conway held sway in the village school.
He taught us to rhyme and he taught us to rule.
We froze in our desks as to Algebra we aspired,
But we thawed out again as we read by the fire.
Oh goodnight Ballivor, I'll sleep in Trim.

Tom Conway was a wise and learned man who was approaching the end of his teaching career when I moved into the senior end of the school. He and his wife Margaret (who taught in Coolronan N.S.) produced a brilliant family of doctors, teachers, a pharmacist, a broadcaster (Medhbh, who became my boss in RTÉ and is responsible for my composition *Goodnight Ballivor, I'll Sleep in Trim*) and an astronomer (Máire, whom their neighbour Mrs Dixon described as a 'Shtargazer'). We soon got used to Master Conway's quirks – how he went up and down on his heels as he spoke; how he would occasionally lapse into nostalgic digressions ('when I was in Marseilles …') and how he would bode the mood of the day when he dispatched Micky Fagan with his tobacco knife to 'cut a good sally-rod.'

We chanted our multi-purpose tables –

Eight sevens are fifty-six; pence, four and eightpence
Eight eights are sixty-four; pence, five and fourpence

We learned of the chief towns and industries of each county. There would *always* be pottery in Arklow, sugar making in Tuam, shoe laces in Ennis. Nothing would ever change. From our English reader came the story of Hans, the brave little Dutch boy who saved his country by keeping his finger in the dyke. We learned by heart (interesting expression!) the stirring 'March to Kinsale' by Aubrey de Vere –

> *O'er many a river bridged with ice*
> *Through many a vale with snowdrifts dumb*
> *Past quaking fen and precipice*
> *The princes of the North are come.*

In arithmetic we struggled with the Unitary Method, Simple Interest and Area. Never were so many rooms needing carpeting, walls needing papering or gardens needing pathways. Mental Arithmethic was important because it formed part of the Primary Certificate examination to which we all aspired ...

> *Find the cost of a gross of eggs @ $4\frac{1}{2}$ d. each.*
> *What is .55 of £120 ?*

There were other examinations looming – the annual catechetical test by the diocesan examiner –

> *Q. What is Purgatory?*
> *A. It's a place in England, Father.* (How right he probably was ...)

And the Big One – the Confirmation Examination where it was decided if you were a '1', a '2' or a '3'. If you were a '1', you went before Dr Kyne, the Bishop of Meath, to be asked a question – *What is perfect contrition?* – be signed with chrism and given a stroke on the cheek to indicate you were a 'strong and perfect Christian'. I have a clear memory of sitting up in bed, sobbing my way through The Apostle's Creed, in anticipation of it being examined in school the following day.

School was also the distribution centre for the most popular reading material of the day – the *Messenger of the Sacred Heart* and the *Far East*. While we all enjoyed Pudsy Ryan's column in the latter we were enjoined by the Master not to attempt to spell like Pudsy –

... a speshal visiter kame to our skool ...

Master Conway raised our academic standards somewhat higher than Primary Certificate level. We aspired to Algebra and Basic Geometry, and I remember struggling with a very difficult Irish reader – *Cúdar agus Scéalta Eile* – with Master Flood.

Many years later the 'old school' where my generation had laboured and learned became the 'New Hall' and was touted in the local press as the 'Mecca of the Midlands', where undoubtedly romance would blossom. Again the crowds assembled. Again the problem of the dance floor arose – how to make it slippery. This time the bright spark came up with a new solution. Soapflakes. At least this showed a greater awareness of health and safety. So the Mecca was thronged and the revelry rose. And the lemonade and the tea (and probably the sweat) were spilled. And the revellers whipped up a froth of Lux bubbles and suds as they whirled around the floor ... that same floor which ten years earlier we had sprinkled with water and tea leaves and swept each evening after school ... Master Conway organised a rota of *lucht scuabtha* (sweepers) among the village children who hadn't far to travel home. How we could have done with some Lux soapflakes then!

I gCuimhne an Mháistir

The Master's dead.

D'ye remember how his pocket-knife
Boded the humour of the day?
A cut of plug would guarantee
a reminiscence of
'When I was in Marseilles'.
But when Mickey Fagan was sent to cut a sally switch
Then you might look to your Euclid, Glenanaar
Or Cúrsaí an Lae.

The Master's dead.

'Didn't he reach a grand age?'
'Aye. Eighty-nine.'
'Sure he must have taught the whole village in his time.'
Indeed.
When we laid him to rest in Ballivor soil –
Returning to the scene of a lifetime's toil –
I thought
Surely these are his pupils' children's children
That line the way.
And surely we should say
The Master lives.

Slán abhaile, a Mháistir.

In my last years at the school, Christo Flood and Ned Carey succeeded Master Conway. They prepared us for County Council Scholarship examinations – or rather those few of us who aspired to go on to secondary education. And so there were new horizons to be discovered –

> *Write a note on two of the following:*
> *The Black Country, Spitsbergen, The Kiel Canal, Sicily,*
> *Marseilles* (thank you, Master Conway).

A cherished memory of that time is of a pencil case. My sister Kay, who was training as a nurse in Dublin, brought me a present from the Big City. A pencil case. Not any old pencil case. This was a wooden double-decker pencil case. The beautifully embossed lid slid out of a groove to reveal two pencil compartments and two smaller ones to hold an eraser and nibs. Then – presto! – you swivelled the upper deck to reveal a lower deck with secret compartments! A small thing maybe, but I cherished it with inordinate pride, just like Huw in Richard Llewellyn's *How Green Was My Valley* –

> *Solomon never felt for his storehouse as I felt for that little box ... To have pens and pencils and the tools of writing all your own, to see them and feel them in your fingers ready to do anything you tell them, to have them in a little house fit for them as good friends of yours, such is sweet pleasure indeed, and never-ending. For you open gently and take what you want, and careful in closing again, and you look at it before you start your work, and all the time a happy fullness inside you that sometimes will make you put out your hand to touch it as though to bless, so good you feel with it ...*

(Twenty-five years later I would be honoured to meet Richard Llewellyn and record him reading the above passage for radio.)

There is a grainy grey photograph of the 'Senior School' taken on a grey morning in the grey surroundings of the schoolyard in 1954. The newly arrived young principal (Ned Carey) peeps shyly out from the school porch along with his young son. There we all are – thirty-five of us – the grey children of the grey fifties. There's Betty Dempsey, to whom I professed undying love at the age of eleven ... her sister Berna and Teresa Mitchell, both dead from cancer. Camillus Maye is the only one dressed for what is obviously a raw spring day – buttoned-up overcoat and woollen scarf. There are the twins Eileen and Agnes McKay who live in Parkstown House and whose parents must be very wealthy – they have *two* wireless sets. To my right is my best pal John Joe Cummins, shoulders hunched, unaccustomed to posing for photographs – as we all are. And there's Maureen McGearty with the bow in her hair. Maureen and I were joint winners of a competition to compose a prayer to St Columbanus, the parish patron. First prize from the curate – a rosary beads each.

We are the grey children, posing self-consciously in the schoolyard, but every single one of us is *smiling* ...

Schoolyard

A rough gravelled yard
A turf-shed
And two pine trees
From which we tapped resin
To harden our palms
Against the Master's stick
(or so we thought ...)
The yard at playtime
Was a mayhem of games
– Football, tig, hide-and-seek -
(Hide WHERE for God's sake?)
The footballers bullied their way
Into possession
Brutally chasing a rag-ball
Until it was irretrievably lost
In Dixon's jungle-garden.
When rain stopped play
We crowded into the turf-shed
And there
Amid the horseplay
We breathed in turf-mould
And exchanged fleas and germs.

14 Seasons in the Sun

A line from a 1970s song goes – *We had joy, we had fun, we had seasons in the sun*. There was a seasonal or cyclical element to the fun we had in my childhood. It was simple, unsophisticated fun by today's standards, but there was just as much daring and delight in it for us. Let's start in the autumn.

The orchards are ripe and inviting. Into Dr McQuaid's or Jim Newman's, stuff your pockets and jumper with the juiciest of the crop and make good your escape (it wouldn't look well for the Sergeant's son to be caught). Halloween comes around. Indoors we play snap-apple, dive into a basin of water to rescue a threepenny-bit with our teeth and watch out for the ring in the brack. Outdoors we play practical jokes – knock on doors and run away. Johnny Dempsey scares us all, arising from the Protestant graveyard, draped in a sheet.

The evenings are drawing in. We pursue indoor hobbies like stamp-collecting, through which we learn of 'faraway places with strange-sounding names' like Madagascar, Mauritius, Tonga. We play cards – Beggar My Neighbour, Snap, Old Maid. We listen to the radio, of course, from the sedate Sean Bunny on Radio Éireann to the relentless adventures of Dick Barton, Special Agent, on BBC Radio. There's Radio Luxembourg too, for the pop charts of the day, and the sponsored programmes such as Cadburys – *'Join the C-Cubs, and get your membership badge and secret code ...'* There are comics to be read – the *Beano, Dandy* and *Radio Fun*. How many cow pies will

Desperate Dan eat this week? Korky the Cat is a howl! And as for The Falcon – 'police can't catch him; all crooks fear him! ...' During our altarboy days my brother Noel and I would 'play Mass' – acting out the ritual we observed each day on the altar. We would hold up a biscuit – *Hoc est enim corpus meum* – or an eggcup of water – *Hic est enim calix sanguinis mei* – while our mother looked on, daring to hope for a priest in the family. There would be occasional ghost stories told (every Protestant house had a ghost).

Winter is upon us now. Freezing nights when you buried yourself under the blankets, trying desperately to get warm and trying not to aggravate the chilblains that tormented your fingers and toes. Before going to bed sneak out and throw a couple of buckets of water on the street – tomorrow night you will have a spectacular slide which you can negotiate on your hunkers on hobnailed boots (to be honest I was more a spectator myself! Coward!). Hurry up before the Sergeant spoils the fun by spreading salt on the slide to prevent motor accidents. And then the snow! Snowmen, snowfights, even snowdrinks – a handful of snow in a glass of milk! I have no memory at all of 'White '47' – the great 'snow-in' that lasted from late January to mid-March – but then I was only five.

Christmas was not the commercial circus it is today. A visit to Santa at Clerys on 8 December and then fingers crossed. The Christmas stocking might reveal a board game (Snakes and Ladders or Ludo) or maybe a six-gun (with caps of course) or a carpentry set. A sponge ball, a toy car or some sweets would add to our delight. Eithne Conway tells a lovely story of her neighbour Mrs Dixon pointing out Santa's footprints in the soot of the hearth (carefully made earlier with a pitchfork).

As the 'cock's step' progressed on January evenings we would venture outdoors once more. Hostilities would resume in the backyard between Noel and myself under the guise of football or hurling. The inevitable disputes, sulks and walk-offs would follow and Mrs Reynolds would undoubtedly add to her collection of hurling balls. As spring advanced we moved to the football field when preparations began for the coming season. We practised in the hope of making the juvenile team (a futile hope in my case) and stayed on to watch 'the men' – hardy seniors like Paddy Dixon, Jim Dargan or 'The Black' Doyle – kick about. We would be honoured to retrieve the ball from behind the goals or out of the ditch for our heroes.

It was birdnesting time now. We spent hours of anticipation and delight in finding the nest of a thrush or a blackbird. You could marvel at the watertight construction of the nest and the beauty of the freckled blue-green eggs, but don't touch them! – or else the mother will forsake the nest. Once Noel intruded on a pigeon's nest, brought home a scrawny fledgeling and reared it himself as a pet. A successful experiment until 'Pidgy' came off worst in a collision with the Ballina bus.

Early summer and the fields and hedgerows are aflame with flowers. We collect primroses and cowslips to adorn the May altar that is a feature of nearly every home. The street echoes with our game-cries – 'tig', 'hide-and-seek', 'ring-a-ring-a-rosy', 'the big ship sails'. Skipping and ball games are enjoyed in yards and gardens. Cowboys chase Indians down alleyways on imaginary pinto ponies and 'finish them off' in the canyon with bloodcurdling whoops (men only of course). There was a particularly unusual and dangerous game that we learned from the children of a travelling 'fit-up' company. It was called simply Cat. A short (4–6 inches) piece of wood (cat) – usually pared at both ends – was placed on a block, jutting out over the edge. You then hit the 'cat' with a long stick or hurley. It flew into the air. Your opponents tried to catch it and get you 'out' (as in cricket). If they failed, you measured the distance the cat travelled in hurley lengths and thus amassed a score. Most parents banned this game as the 'cat' could fly anywhere and cause serious injury, particularly when – as in cricket – you moved your fielders in close to catch the 'cat'.

High summer now, and if you wanted to be cool and macho you went 'in the bares' i.e. barefoot. All very fine until you stubbed a toe, developed a stone bruise (requiring a bread poultice if it went septic) or stood on molten tar. The school holidays came and you spent days just 'out' – exploring a wood, jumping ditches, wandering freely. There was work to be done too – helping out on the bog (but playing there too), saving the hay (but oh, the jaunts on the hay bogey!) and the endless drawing of water from the pump – for both man and beast. One play session in the bog almost proved fatal for me. My siblings and I were running up and down a dry channel when I went too near the edge and slipped into a boghole. I was going down for the third time when my father and Jim Rickard pulled me out … I was about six and have had a healthy respect for water ever since.

A hot day (and of course there seem to have been many hot days) would lure us to the Stoneyford river to splash and frolic among the cowpat-infested waters. June 29th was Bonfire Night on Fr Farrell's 'island' in Walsh's Big Meadow. It was also the feast of Saints Peter and Paul and a holyday of obligation in those days. Summer meant the football season when we cheered on our heroes against the 'Barmbracks' from Ballinabrackey, or Young Irelands, or Navan O'Mahonys. And hopefully the county team would do well against arch-enemies Louth or Cavan. Micheál O'Hehir's voice carried from our windowsill down the quiet Sunday street. And if we won, all was well with the world.

In August, the mushrooms came. We would set off in the dewy morning for Walsh's Big Meadow, and – hard though the mushrooms tried to hide in sodden grass – we were up to their tricks and would march home triumphantly with several hanks of mushrooms, threaded on *tráithníns*. Put them on the hob with a little knob of butter on each. A sprinkle of salt as they sizzled. No taste will ever come near.

Autumn was here again and school re-opened. A new class, new books and copies to be covered in spare wallpaper or strong brown paper that had been diligently saved for this purpose. The blackberries glutted in the hedgerows and we stuffed ourselves on the way home from school. We might also be dispatched with cans to pick that luscious fruit for jam or tart-making, and if it seemed we took a long time to fill the cans, our purple-stained lips told why.

The ankle-deep leaves on the pathway outside the Protestant church became the material for amazing 'leaf houses' – for the girls, of course. McLaughlin's haybarn was the scene of a potentially dangerous adventure. We tunnelled our way through the solid wall of hay. Exciting fun until Janey Doyle dramatically got stuck on a bend far into the tunnel. She was rescued and that was the end of the adventure. The evenings were drawing in once more. The dark (pre-electricity) street was quiet again, but Halloween was coming ...

15   Street Games

A child of the twenty-first century would find it hard to believe that the PlayStation of fifty or sixty years ago was the 'hoop' – a discarded bicycle wheel, preferably tyreless, bowled and controlled by the bowler's stick. You drove the hoop endlessly up and down the street, deftly negotiating obstacles, doing stylish arcs and circles, 'braking' and slowing, all by dexterous use of the little stick. It was intense fun, but you could 'park' your hoop and take a break before embarking on further adventures.

> *Molly I'd love to be rolling your hoop,*
> *Rolling your hoop, rolling your hoop,*
> *Molly I'd love to be rolling your hoop*
> *Down by the country gardens.*

The simple chasing game of Tig and the more elaborate Chain Tig were the most common of the street games (although you couldn't be 'It' if you showed fingers crossed on both hands and shouted 'crossed legs'). Races were common in the schoolyard – be they 'straight', 'three-legged' or 'potato and spoon' (eggs were too precious!). On the street, the girls played Ring-a-Ring-a-Rosy; another circle game –

> *Around the grey gravel the grass grows green,*
> *Ever a lady fit to be seen,*

Washed in milk, dried in silk,
We all bow down ...

Four-Corner Fool ('fool' in the centre tries to catch others in the corners swapping places), Wallflowers and –

The big ship sails through the alley, alley-o,
The alley, alley-o, the alley, alley-o,
The big ship sails through the alley, alley-o
On the last day of November.

which usually ended in mayhem and laughter.

Games like London Bridge is Falling Down, In and Out Goes Mary Bluebell and I Have a Little Dog involved chasing a chosen one in and out through the circle of children –

I have a little dog
And he won't bite you
Or you, or you, but
He will bite YOU.

Playing Shop usually involved boys and girls. Imagination was given free rein and mud became butter, sand became sugar, stones wrapped in coloured papers became sweets and cigarette packets and other cartons were recycled. You paid for your goods with the 'money' of broken china.

Ball games abounded – from the straightforward DONKEY to others which required more dexterity and were accompanied by rhymes.

Doctor Kelly
Broke his belly
Sliding down
A heap of jelly.

Queenie eye-o
Who has the ball?
Is she small or is she tall?

One, two, three
My mother caught a flea.
She put it in the teapot
To make a cup of tea.
The flea jumped out
My mother let a shout
And in came my father
With his shirt hanging out.

The girls loved skipping and again had several rhymes to accompany skipping games – Goosey, Goosey Gander; Teddy Bear, Teddy Bear; I'll Tell My Ma; Cobbler, Cobbler; Two Little Dicky Birds and –

There was an old man
And his name was Dan
He lived in the bottom
Of an old tin can.
He had a pair of slippers
He turned them into kippers
And they all lived together
In the old tin can.

The boys might prefer Hide and Seek or the more macho I'm the King of the Castle or – in season (early spring) – the more sedate Marbles. They might also try to disrupt the skipping games …

So you want to know the time? Take the seed head of a dandelion. Say 'one o'clock'. Blow the seeds. 'Two o'clock.' Blow again. And so on until the last seed is gone. Whatever time you have reached, that's the time it is. Simple! A disbeliever could reply –

The dandelion puff is a queer little clock
It doesn't say tick and it doesn't say tock
It hasn't a cuckoo and it hasn't a chime
And I really don't think it will tell you the time.

If, on the other hand, you want your fortune told ... Collect some stalks of grass or ears of corn and pluck a seed for each answer, repeating each verse until one seed remains. Wherever you are in the verse, that's your destiny –

1. *What will your husband be?*
   Tinker, tailor, soldier, sailor,
   Rich man, poor man, beggarman, thief.
2. *What sort of home will you have?*
   A big house, a little house, a pigsty, a barn.
3. *What sort of ring will you wear?*
   Copper, lead, gold, silver.
4. *What will you wear to your wedding?*
   Silk, satin, muslin, rags.
5. *What footwear?*
   Boots, shoes, slippers, clogs.
6. *What will you have for wedding cake?*
   Half a loaf, a whole loaf, a sweet cake, a bun.
7. *How will you travel to your wedding?*
   Car, bus, wheelbarrow, dray.
8. *How many children will you have?*
   Five, ten, fifteen, twenty ...

A variety of rhymes was employed to pick sides for a game or to decide who was 'It' i.e. the chaser. There was the politically incorrect (and of course today unacceptable) –

Eeny, meeny, miney, moe
Catch a nigger by the toe
If he squeals let him go
O-U-T spells out
And out you must go!

Others included –

> *Icky, ocky, porter bottle*
> *Out jumps cork!*

(repeated until one child is left as 'It');

and the somewhat rude -

> *I think, I think*
> *I smell a stink*
> *I think, I think*
> *I do*
> *I think, I think*
> *I smell a stink*
> *I think, I think*
> *It's YOU!*

Clapping games –

> *Mrs D – Mrs I*
> *Mrs FFI*
> *Mrs C – Mrs U*
> *Mrs LTY*

Guessing games, tug of war without a rope (we held on to each other) and *Red Rover* (two opposing lines – a child from one side tries to break through the opposing line). There was quite simply a wealth of games to choose from. As well as entertaining us, they enriched us socially – and we never heard of the word 'obesity'! We were also enriched by the language of the street – not just the game rhymes but the jibes, jeers and smart remarks that were part of life –

> *Cowardy, cowardy custard*
> *Dip your head in mustard.*

Tell-tale tattler
Buy a penny rattler.

Shake hands brother
You're a rogue and I'm another.

Rain, rain, go away
Come again another day.

What are you looking at?
Not much.
Look in the mirror
And you'll see less …

Janey Mac,
Me shirt is black
What'll I do for Sunday?
Go to bed
And cover your head
And don't get up till Monday.

What's your name?
Butter and crame [cream]

Skinnymalink
Melodeon Legs
Umbrella Feet

If – if – if -
Only for if, the sky would fall.

Open your mouth
And shut your eyes
And see what God
Will give you.

April Fool is past and gone
You're the fool to carry it on.

Goodnight, sleep tight,
I hope the bugs don't bite.

16 Serving God

At Mass on Easter Sunday morning
Fr Farrell intoned the dues with warning
'One shilling each the following – Thomas Dunne,
Moyfeigher'
While Michael Leddy de-waxed his ears ...
O goodnight, Ballivor, I'll sleep in Trim.

Fr Patrick Farrell dominated Ballivor for forty-two years – literally and metaphorically. Known as 'The Big Man', he was a six-foot six-inch colossus who strode about the village, his black cassock billowing in the breeze. Together with his stern countenance he presented a formidable sight to any youngster who encountered him while he went about reading his breviary.

'Recite the Memorare!' or 'What is commanded by the fourth commandment?' he might bark, and woe betide you if you stumbled through the reply or – worse still – failed to reply. The least you might expect was a verbal scolding. I am told he had a sense of humour but I had no experience of it. Fr Farrell drove an imposing black Ford V8 car. When he ultimately sold it to Paddy Dixon, Paddy bravely suggested a 'luck penny', as would be the custom in cattle dealing. Fr Farrell reached into his pocket and produced a penny which he proffered to the bold 'Stonewall'.

As a child, my dealings with The Big Man were as an altar boy, to which service I was inducted at a young age. It was an induction on several fronts. There were rituals and practices to be observed and learned. There was the strange language of service – Latin – which we learned and parrotted without understanding a single word. Even the English language associated with church ritual was strange and novel. As I donned a soutane and surplice in the sacristy, I was bemused by the array of drawers above the table where the priest dressed. Each drawer was labelled with a mysterious word – palls, purifiers, vestments, cinctures, amices, stoles, pyx, corporals in use and corporals in reserve (was there a secret war going on?). Elsewhere there was a tabernacle, a monstrance, a thurible with incense. There was a whole new language to be learned.

Latin was a major step further into the realm of language but even if it was meaningless to an eight-year-old, to me its rhythms and cadences held an immense fascination. Later when I studied it in secondary school I enjoyed its logic and its connection with English and it became my favourite subject, but for now to roll *'Quia tu es, Deus, fortitudo mea: quare me repulisti, et quare tristes incedo, dum affligit me, inimicus?'* off the tongue was a thrilling challenge. We made the best fist we could of this strange language. For years Johnny Dempsey got away with *Dominus go-biscuits ...*

Of even greater importance was knowing when to ring the bell (in this case a great brass 'mushroom' which we delighted in belting with a wooden mallet), when to bring up the wine and water, when to present the thurible etc. Fr Farrell would be very impatient if you missed your cue. Other duties included bringing the offertory collection plates into the sacristy. For me those plates overflowing with sixpenny and threepenny bits were too big a temptation. Snatch a handful of them and stuff them quickly into your pocket. *Mea culpa, mea culpa, mea maxima culpa ... Ideo precor ... orare pro me ad Dominum Deum nostrum ...*

There were, of course, legal opportunities for financial gain open to an altar server. A wedding or a funeral usually meant a generous tip. Those were the days of funeral offerings, when the priest stood before a table draped with a linen cloth and those attending the funeral came forward with their 'Mass offerings' for the deceased. When all had paid, the altar boys gathered the four corners of the tablecloth and made off with 'the take' to the sacristy ... No. No. *Don't even think of it. Et ne nos inducas in tentationem ...*

(As recently as the 1970s, funeral offerings were still taken up in Monaghan. At my uncle's funeral the priest was flanked by two local men to identify the offerers.) '*I never seen a take as big as that before. Begod, the Canon'll have a new car on the strength of it.*' (Taken from my novel, *Generations of the Moon*)

For those who could afford it, a 'Solemn High Mass' was the ultimate send-off for the deceased. Seven priests might celebrate a High Mass. Seven priests would have to be recompensed. The actual funeral was held later in the afternoon because the 'fasting from midnight' rule for Holy Communion meant that refreshment was needed after the long funeral Mass. Apart from funeral offerings, church offerings were collected through the year (Easter, Christmas etc.) and as indicated in the verse above, were read out with measure and intent by Fr Farrell, beginning with the largest offerings (a pound, maybe) and working right down (to the shame of many) to the mites of shillings and sixpences.

An altar server's life was a busy one. Apart from morning Mass, one could be summoned for Benediction, Evening Devotions, Holy Hours, Stations of the Cross ... In the latter instance, being a candle bearer was fraught with difficulties – avoiding the hot wax dripping down as you made your way around the stations and avoiding the embarrassment of having your candle extinguished by a draught from the door caused by a late arrival (or indeed an early departure when Fr Farrell wasn't looking). The eighth station always puzzled me, when Fr Farrell solemnly intoned – 'Compassionate your Saviour, thus cruelly treated ...' What was this compassion anyway and why did it eat our Saviour?

Equally puzzling was the ceremony known as 'churching', when a woman who recently had a baby had to come to the altar to be 'churched'. It seemed and sounded almost as if she had done wrong – but what could she have done wrong?

Fr Farrell died in the Holy Year of 1950 and was replaced by Fr William Kiernan – a forceful and no-nonsense parish priest. He organised a major clean-up of the church grounds and persuaded a visitor to the village – a Dr Sean Coghlan – to donate the beautiful Earley-made stained glass window depicting the Crucifixion to the church. It cost two thousand pounds – a very considerable sum at the time. Fr Kiernan was very much the driving force in bringing electrification to the village. We had curates also. Fr Colm Murtagh initiated the idea of an altar boys' outing by bringing a carload of us to the Town Hall in Trim to see the local musical society's production of Romberg's *The New Moon*. For all of us it would be an important introduction to theatre. There was also Fr Cuffe who – as recorded in *Fair Day* – caused me a severe loss of earnings on one of those days. Finding he had no-one to serve Mass, he marched out, grabbed the first altar boy he met by the ear and dragged me into the church, muttering, 'You cannot serve God and Mammon'.

17 The Bog

In his poem 'A Drover', Padraic Colum referred to our county as 'Meath of the pastures' and while most of the county is indeed lush grassland, the Great Bog of Allen encroaches from the western side and 'the bog' was an important part of Ballivor's economic and social life for generations. 'Ballivor's lonely moors' (as one ballad described the bog) included the townlands of Coolronan, Carronstown, Robinstown and Cloneycavan. (The latter recently gained notoriety worldwide when it gave up 'Cloneycavan Man' – a two-thousand-year-old skeleton so well preserved that he still had his hair gel! There is no truth in the rumour that he was a casualty of a particularly vicious Feis Cup Final!)

It was common in the 1940s and 1950s for a family to rent a bank of turf from a local owner and then 'save' the turf for the winter. Sergeant Quinn rented a plot each year from John Kelly, whom he christened 'Seán T.' after the president of the day. It wasn't just a business arrangement. My parents would regularly visit the Kellys in their little tin-roofed cottage in the bog on Sunday afternoons in summer. It was the most welcoming of places. To my childhood eye, Kelly's house seemed to be at the end of the world. The potholed bog road petered out at Kellys. There were four children in the household – Johnny, Lena, Mary Ann and Patsy. I have written about Johnny elsewhere; he always had a twinkle of devilment in his eye and would turn a blind one when we children would gorge ourselves on the sweetest of gooseberries in Kellys' garden.

> *We cut the turf on Coolronan bog,*
> *Spread it, footed it, an awful slog;*
> *But 'twas a day off school, so there was no hurry,*
> *And we rode home in style in Jim Rickard's lorry.*
> *Oh goodnight Ballivor, I'll sleep in Trim.*

In the main, the bog was about work – hard, back-breaking work. My father might hire a man to 'give him a day on the bog' but the children were pressed into service too – to spread, foot and ultimately clamp the turf. We would be ferried out after school (or occasionally given a day off school) but the novelty soon wore off when we toiled beneath a boiling sun and the hunger pangs gnawed after only an hour (though it seemed like several hours). Eventually we were given a break for tea and sandwiches on the bog or back in Seán T.'s *árus* – and never did food and drink taste so sweet. My father's delight was a mug of buttermilk, but no matter how desperate my thirst, I couldn't face that particular beverage.

It wasn't all work however. We were given the freedom of the bog to run wild and play (shenanigans which nearly caused my drowning – see *Seasons in the Sun*). Fifty years later Johnny Kelly would point out a tree 'which you and Noel used to climb and answer the cuckoo!' Those childhood days in the bog eventually found their way into my first children's novel – *The Summer of Lily and Esme …*

> *The room was cool and dark, a welcome refuge from the*
> *noonday heat. 'Let ye take your ease while the kettle is*
> *boiling,' Lena said, offering them a glass of diluted*
> *orange drink each. Alan savoured every drop that slipped*
> *down his parched throat. The kettle soon began to sing*
> *on the open hearth. Alan was intrigued by the novelty of*
> *the fire with its various crooks suspended from the dark*

chimney. Lena hummed to herself as she busily filled two cans of tea from the huge black kettle. Nobody spoke. It was just what Alan and Lisa wanted: a cool, peaceful and welcoming place.

'Off ye go now,' said Lena, securing the lids on the cans. 'The hotter the tea is on a day like this the better. And there's a little extra. Soda bread hot off the griddle! 'Tis buttered and all. Your grandad loves that, Lisa. Goodbye now. God bless ye.'

Alan didn't want to leave.

'Come on, zombie!' Lisa called.

'Thank you,' Alan said. 'We'll call again.'

'Do indeed. A soul gets lonely out here at times.'

They hurried back as quickly as the full cans would allow them. Alan opened up the hold-all. Mrs Grehan had gauged their hunger well. The bag was teeming with an assortment of sandwiches: tomato, egg, ham and his own favourite, cucumber. The four ate in silence. Never did food taste so good. Alan wolfed the sandwiches and savoured the tea.

'God bless Lena,' Tom said at last. 'No-one can make tea like her.'

''Tis the spring water,' Heels mumbled through a sandwich.

'And she has a surprise for you,' Lisa added, unwrapping the soda bread. Tom's face lit up like a child's at Christmas time. 'Lord save us, Heels. We'll do no more

work after this.' The soda bread was still warm and
generously soaked in butter. It was delicious.
THE SUMMER OF LILY AND ESME

As with his work on the land, my father's work on the bog was
meticulous and thorough. Johnny Kelly recalled how the
Sergeant would start cleaning the high bank as early as the end
of March and would be bringing the turf home at the end of
May 'when everyone else would be only starting!' It was all high
bank work then. I can still hear the slice and suck of the slane
and can marvel at the glistening sods flying through the air to
land in perfect alignment on the heather or, as Johnny put it, 'He
took that big deal tree as his mark and threw the sods down like
drills of potatoes – the grandest that was ever seen'. Once there
was a fire on the bog and the Sergeant worked through the night
to move his turf to safety. Home then, with a full load on Jim
Rickard's lorry. The turf was saved. Winter warmth was assured,
neatly stacked in the shed behind the house.

There were other visitors to Coolronan. During the
'Emergency', soldiers were sent to harvest turf – eighteen
hundred of them according to Johnny Kelly. They set up a huge
camp in the bog and were amazed to emerge at bugle call on
their first morning to find a carpet of snow on the ground.
Amazed, because it was the month of May, 1940. The soldiers
were cutting turf to supply government buildings and essential
services in Dublin. I have a memory of the long ricks of turf
stacked high along the main road of the Phoenix Park. The
soldiers gradually integrated themselves into the local society –
playing football against the Meath team in Ballivor (Boiler
McGuinness's last match!), attending dances (I'm sure a number
of marriages happened as a result) and giving their custom to
local pubs – probably giving my father occasional headaches!
For five or six years, the soldiers were a major part of life in the
village and the bog.

And when the soldiers departed, another army took over the
bog. Bord na Móna – the state turf board – began operations in

Robinstown in 1946 under the chief engineer Mr Filgate. The giant peat machines – the 'baggers' – advanced across Ballivor's lonely moors, leaving row upon row of neatly cut turf in hitherto unimaginable quantities. A railway was laid across the bog to ferry both men and turf to and from the central depot. Lorries rumbled through the village bearing Bord na Móna peat to distant parts. Ballivor had an industry. The bog would never be the same again.

The Bord na Móna operation created major employment opportunities for local men. Every morning a small army of cyclists made its way through the village and out the Robinstown road. There was also opportunity for occasional employment for young men – my Trim friend Albert McGonagle and I envisaged earning a small fortune one summer. We would be paid *seven shillings and sixpence* for footing a 'square' of turf. We dreamed of being millionaires as we set off with the *men* on the bog train. When we saw the size of the 'square', the dream began to fade rapidly. Our millionaire career lasted one day.

In a corner of Coolronan there are raspberry gardens, possibly the remnants of a one-time commercial enterprise. Eithne Conway has vivid memories of being despatched with her siblings to fill two three-quart cans with the delicious fruit. The rule was: don't eat a raspberry until the first can is full. *Then* you could put a handful of berries into your bread and butter sandwiches. A true feast! You struggled to fill the second can, but when you did, you had the guarantee of delicious jam till the next season. That was grand until the end of the war when jam was scarce and – as Eithne puts it – 'the townies came from Trim in droves and, not knowing the gardens like we did, they traipsed all over them, destroying the lovely bushes'.

In those same gardens in August 2005 an annual Mass on the bog was initiated. It was a wonderful concept – celebrating the importance of the bog in the lives of generations of Ballivor people. It was a community celebration. When Mass was over, car boots were opened and picnics ensued. There was conversation, laughter, music and dance. It was a very special occasion which proved the reverence and love people have for this most sacred place where they would find – in the words of Patrick Kavanagh –

> *That beautiful, beautiful, beautiful God*
> *Was breathing His love by a cut-away bog.*

A few days later I penned the following lines –

The Bog Beatitudes

Blessed are the slanesmen,
> *for they have sliced their way through our past.*
Blessed are the catchers,
> *for their sure summer hands have won the winter prize.*

Blessed are the barrowers,
> *for they have borne our burdens to the higher ground.*
Blessed are the spreaders,
> *for their backs have ached in the bristling heather.*

Blessed are the footers,
> *for they have invited the drying wind and sun.*
Blessed are the clampers,
> *for they have built the ricks, tidy and trim.*

Blessed are the tea-and-sandwich-makers,
> *for they have quenched our hunger and our thirst.*
Blessed are the singers,
> *for their voices have lifted our weary hearts.*

Blessed are the lorrymen,
> *for they have filled our sheds with winter warmth.*
Blessed are the turfmakers,
> *for they have glimpsed heaven and the face of God.*

18 A Day to Remember

On 19 July 1996 I made a journey into the past. I went back to Coolronan Bog to record a radio documentary – A Day on the Bog. *Johnny Kelly's nephew, John Joe Hiney, had assured me he would assemble a team to recreate a day on the bog – cutting turf by hand. It was for me the most enthralling and fulfilling of days. It was as if I had never been away or had been transported fifty years back in time. The following is an attempt to recapture that memorable day in print.*

I see the familiar stooped figure of Johnny Kelly in the distance.

'How are ye living?' he greets me. 'You woke me this morning at five o'clock.'

'I woke you?'

'Yeh. I turned on the radio and your programme was on. So I said to myself that man is coming today – I had better get ready! I was out here on the high bank, cleaning it off at six o'clock in the morning. And do you know what, John? It was the loveliest morning ever. I had a view of the whole county, with nothing moving bar a hare or a pheasant. It reminded me of a June morning years ago during the war, when English troops tried to take back France from the Germans. I could hear the bugle going up in the army camp as the sun was rising like a huge red ball in the sky ...'

We meet the next man on the team – slanesman Frank Kelly.

J.Q.:   Another Kelly!

Frank: Sure the place is polluted with Kellys.

Frank produces a slane and he and Johnny argue over its maker. It could be a 'Burke' or a 'Boylan' or a 'Hesnan'. It's most likely a 'Burke', they agree. Frank explains the purpose of the cow's horn fitted to the top of the slane-handle; to prevent it from chafing against the body. For a right-handed slanesman you need the cow's left horn and vice versa for a left-hander.

Frank: I have an ould 'scup' here too but we won't need it on the high bank.

Johnny: Oh gouta that, Frankeen! What's it made of at all?

Frank: The hubcap of an old Volkswagen fixed to a shovel handle.

Johnny: I bought a plastic basin to make a 'scup'. It's at home with the dog in the shed!

Frank explains that the 'scup' is used to ladle out water that accumulates when working on the low bank. It transpires he is an avid collector of old tools and machines. He produces a little tin box. Inside is a tiny sod of turf wrapped in a certificate that declares it the first sod cut when the county council began turfcutting in 1941. The slanesman was Jack Kelly, Frank's father.

Johnny: Well, there's no doubt – we have plenty of slanes and no workmen!

The workmen do come. Pat Kelly, Frank's brother, is the catcher and wheeler, using the distinctive turf barrow he made himself.

John Joe Hiney helps also. The work begins. Frank gets into a
steady rhythm. He comes across a layer of *cíob*.

Johnny: That *cíob* is a kind of weed that wouldn't wither in
two thousand years. It's a villain!

Frank: You have to stab the blade of the slane in and twist it
with force of your arms – all in the one movement.

Johnny: When you hear that slicing sound, that's the slane
singing 'fill me again'!

Frank: Johnny, we forgot the 'yorks' – to tie the trousers
under the knees and allow movement.

Johnny: I have a few bits of twine in the car. Sure – as Micheál
O'Hehir says – 'this game hasn't come to life yet!'

Frank: And I haven't my boots either. You need the nailed
boot to put your own brand on the turf.

Johnny: Sure them is only dancin' shoes you have on today,
Frankeen!

Lena Hiney, Johnny's sister, arrives.

Frank: Come on, Lena. Get to work with that barrow!

Lena: Ah, I'm too old for that, Frankeen!

Frank: Well, I seen the day you could do it – and no mistake!

John Joe Hiney shows how to 'cant' the barrow – let go of the
'bottom' handle when tipping over the barrowload.

Johnny: Isn't it great the way when a *gossoon* is trained when he's young – it never leaves the blood!

Another figure appears, with an accordion on his back.

Frank: Who's that, now?

Johnny: It's Jimeen Murray – with the box.

Frank: Ah Jesus, Murray – would you ever sweeten yourself up? You look more like a fellow coming home from the bog than going to it!

Jimmy provides background music – 'The Old Bog Road' – as the work progresses.

Johnny: That's a grand quality of turf now. You'd know by the grain in it. None of that ould light sponge.

J.Q.: Frank is really flying now!

Frank: Not bad for a fellow with two replacement hips!

Johnny: Good man, Frankeen! They say a right-handed slanesman is best – he's cuttin' away from his heart.

J.Q.: How long would you leave that turf after you 'spread' it, Johnny?

Johnny: About a week, John. Then 'foot' it to let the sun and wind dry it. It'll be ready then in about a month, if the weather is good. Tell us, John, have you an open fire at home in Galway?

J.Q.: Indeed I have.

Johnny: Sure that's the real ass's milk! Bring your ass and cart in a month or so and we'll load you up!

Another figure arrives, dressed in shorts and ready for action.

Johnny: It's Joeen Dempsey from Trim.

J.Q.: Are you on for a bit of work, Joe?

Joe: I'm a left-hander.

Johnny: No bother, Joeen. I have a left-handed slane for you here!

J.Q.: Is this the same Joe Dempsey who used to do Micheál O'Hehir impressions for us in Ballivor years ago?

Joe: One and the same!

As Joe starts cutting, he sings a few verses of the 'Ballivor Football Song'.

J.Q.: Not easy to sing and cut turf at the same time, Joe?

Joe: No. As they would say in Europe, the cohesion isn't there!

The work is in full swing now. The chat and banter continue but there is 'a sight of turf' being cut …

Jimmy: Do you think will Meath beat the Dubs on Sunday week, Joe?

Joe: I don't think so. Too many young lads on the team. It'll be a baptism of fire for them.

Johnny: Sure isn't Redmond not playing for Dublin? And McNally?

Jimmy: That might be only foxin!

Joe: Aye! As I roved out ...

J.Q.: What about a bit of commentary on the 1949 Final, Joe?

Joe: Wait till I get my breath back. I had an ould quadruple job a while back —

J.Q.: A what?

Joe: A quadruple by-pass.

J.Q.: And the fellow behind you has two replacement hips!

Joe: That's the reason! We were the fellows who did the work!

Joe launches into an O'Hehir commentary with an uncanny reproduction of the broadcaster's voice, replete with all the clichés ...

> *Fáilte romhaibh go Páirc an Chrócaigh for the 1949 All-Ireland Final between Cavan, the men from Breifne, seeking their third title in a row, and their near neighbours, Meath. Meath – always the bridesmaid, never the bride! ... The ball is in and the game is on and straight away it's Cavan on the attack. A high dropping ball from the Gunner Brady, but it's cleared by Paddy 'Stonewall' Dixon. On to his captain Brian Smith. A quick pass to Paddy Meegan and it's over the bar ... Paddy Connell at centrefield pulls a ball out of the sky*

*and lofts an equally high ball towards the Cavan goal.
Not sure if the direction is right. This is a 'Fág an
Bealach' but it drops over the bar ... The ball is in the
square – a bit of a schemozzle in there but Bill Halpenny
gets a fist to it and it's in the net. IT'S A GOAL! A
GOAL FOR MEATH! ... The kickout lands in the
middle of the field but referee Dan Ryan blows his
whistle and, in a major upset, Meath are All-Ireland
Champions for the very first time! ...*

We cheer Joe just as lustily as we might have cheered in 1949 ...

With impeccable timing Maureen McGearty arrives with
'the tea' – sandwiches, sweet cake, apple tarts and plenty of hot
tea in bottles wrapped in newspaper.

J.Q.: It doesn't get much better than this, Joe?

Joe: It reminds me of that picture – *All That Heaven
Allows*!

The men relax and fall into easy conversation.

Jimmy: Does anyone remember Bozzana?

Joe: Oh Bozzana! Big Andy Elliott would say.

Johnny: He was a great slanesman from over Bracklyn way. A
Frenchman.

Frank: Yeh. Bonanza I used to call him. He had a fierce rivalry
with Mick Walsh – to see which of them could throw
the sods out in chainlink form – like a string of
sausages!

The conversation turns to the local geography.

Jimmy: Isn't that Doire Fliuch over there, Johnny?

Johnny: Aye, and the Braitheas next to it – and on to
           Knockshebane.
           'At Knockshebane I met a man
           Called Rory of the Hill ...'

J.Q.:   What was that about, Johnny?

Johnny: It's about a notorious landlord who evicted a young
           man for not paying his rent. The landlord was coming
           home in his carriage and his driver was told to go easy
           when he came to Knockshebane. When he did this
           your man creeps up behind the landlord and puts a
           Number Four [cartridge] in the back of his head ...

Joe: And where's Scroogawn, Johnny?

Johnny: Just up there, Joeen. That big hill of gravel with the
           oak tree on top. Worth goin' there for a week. They
           say strange things come out at night – but I don't think
           the hotel is open today, Joeen!

Joe: They must start the Sabbath early!

Johnny: And there's Robber's Bush. A fellow called Christy
           Neill lived up there and they say he had his own coffin
           made long before he died!

Jimmy Murray gives us a rendition of *The Corns Song* – the story
of a lovelorn young man and a damsel who suffers with corns.

> *So I took her along by the arm*
> *Till we came to an old wooden stile.*
> *She said, 'me toes are all covered with corns*
> *Would you mind sitting down for a while?'*

Boys, now sure that's what I wanted
　And the moment she sat on my knee
With my arms tugged tightly around her
　I kissed her and gave her a squeeze.

She said 'Young man, you're too forward.
　You should not have kissed me for a while!'
When I said it was the cure for the corns
　Oh bedad, but she screwed up a smile!

So we talked for the rest of the evening
　Till the old village clock it struck ten.
And when I said it was time to be goin'
　'Oh,' says she, 'I've the corns again!'

Refreshed with good food and laughter, the team resumes work. Joe Dempsey tries his hand as the catcher.

Joe:　　Oh, that's the real *cíor* sod now.

J.Q.:　　What's the *cíor* sod, Joe?

Joe:　　It's the real black stuff – after you get through the *cíob* and the ould *spadach*.

Johnny:　Correct, Joeen. That's it.

Frank:　I remember, as a young lad, running three miles from home in the morning to catch a lift to the bog in a cart. Then all day catching turf for two and eightpence a day.

Johnny:　There's two lorryloads of that turf there now lads and you mightn't fret for the winter. And I didn't work yis too hard!

Joe: No, but it was the quality of the 'subs' you brought on!

The 'day on the bog' is over. Frank Kelly puts away his implements with care.

Frank: This is what you do with the slane. Wipe it down, shine it up with a bit of sandpaper and wrap it in a bit of sacking to have it ready for the next day. You NEVER hit it off a rock to clean it. If you do, the slightest 'gimp' will mark every sod you cut. You have to treat it with care. It's a craftsman's tool.

Johnny: Well, good luck lads and thanks. Ye were a great team. Please God, we'll all be alive this time next year. Safe home, lads.

Sadly, the following decade took away four of the team – Johnny Kelly and his sister Lena, Jimmy Murray and Frank Kelly. Somehow I reckon that on a high bank in heaven the four of them are having the craic and the banter. They deserve no less.

19 A Tribute to Johnny Kelly

Graveside Oration – 3 September 1998

My name is John Quinn. I was born in Ballivor, three doors away from the church. I spent the first fourteen years of my life in Ballivor – the most important fourteen years of my life. It is quite incredible the hold that those years and that place have on me. I was 'the sergeant's son', to use the description given by this wonderful man whose passing we mourn and whose life we celebrate – Johnny Kelly.

Johnny 'starred' – and I use that much-abused word deliberately – in two radio documentaries – *Goodnight Ballivor, I'll Sleep in Trim* and *A Day on the Bog*. He didn't 'star' in the Hollywood sense of giving a performance – he was just himself. Over the past few years, people I met in the course of my work have asked me, 'How is Johnny Kelly?' 'I don't know him but I know him, if you know what I mean ... there's someone like him in every parish.' Hopefully there is. And hopefully they are treasured in their communities.

Because Johnny Kelly was a treasure. A *treasure of wisdom* and local lore. He knew the placenames, the names of fields and townlands, the people and their stories ... A *treasure of language*: I recall his inimitable expressions like 'I was so hungry I could eat the sock of a plough'; and 'My people were put out on the soft side of the road ...' A *treasure of civility* and decency and values.

Johnny was part of my childhood. I came regularly – and probably unwillingly! – with my father to save the turf on Johnny's father's bog. My father always referred to Johnny's father (also John) as 'Sean T.' à la the president of the day. It was a great treat at the end of a day's work (although it was probably only a few hours!) to be offered tea and a good big sandwich or a slice of curranty bread in the Kellys' house – that most welcoming and welcome of places. It was an even greater treat to revisit that childhood on tape with Johnny in the Ballivor documentary – to be shown the actual tree that Johnny remembered me climbing to answer the cuckoo ... to be shown the now overgrown 'last pit your father dug'.

When I came back forty years later, it was as if I had never been away. The cup of tea, the sweet cake, the perfectly clear memory. I'm glad I came back and recorded him because – mark my word – Johnny was one of a rare breed. In the age of the soundbyte and the glib comment, he was the master of story. In the age of the fake and the plastic, he was the genuine article, or – to use one of his own memorable expressions – he was 'the real ass's milk'. In the age of fools and foolishness, he was truly wise. Johnny Kelly lived all his life in the bog. He wasn't an 'educated' man, as we use the term, but he had more wisdom in him than many people who hold strings of university degrees.

So we mourn his passing but we rejoice in his memory and in the many ways he touched our lives – through his wit, his sayings, his love of football, his genuine love of life and love of the bog. He was the epitome of the poet's words –

> *Happy the man whose wish and care*
> *A few paternal acres bound*
> *Content to breathe his native air*
> *In his own ground ...*

Johnny was happy. He was content. And I loved him. We all loved him. When I heard of his death on Tuesday, I listened again to some of the tapes I had made with Johnny on that most memorable 'day on the bog'. At the end of the day he stood on his beloved bog with myself and Maureen McGearty, and explained how if the wind was from one direction you could hear the Ballivor bell, from another you could hear the Killyon bell, from another the Killulagh bell, from another the Kildalkey bell and so on – he was surrounded by bells!

Johnny, today you don't need the wind, because I know that all the bells are ringing out joyously to welcome you home. Safe home, Johnny.

20 The Wee Hills I

My father came from a small farm in Co. Monaghan, right up against the Border. The townland was Drumacon, in the parish of Muckno in the barony of Cremorne, about equidistant from Castleblayney and Crossmaglen.

> *From Carrickmacross to Crossmaglen*
> *There are more rogues than honest men.*

My father would often quote those lines in the course of his many visits home to 'the wee hills' – the beautiful drumlin and lake country that is Monaghan. For us, his children, Drumacon was a magical place – a real working farm with horses, cattle, pigs and poultry. The house was cosily surrounded by intriguing stables and stores, a dark and mysterious loft, hayricks in the haggard, an orchard and a flaxpool. A trip to Monaghan was a trip to be savoured, above all else for the kindly and warm company of uncles and aunts.

Hugh Quinn was the eldest of seven children born to Charles and Catherine Quinn. I never knew my grandparents and the only photograph I have of my grandmother is one of her standing in a field with my aunt Katie, looking dour and sad in her 'widow's weeds'. But the same Katie assured me that her mother was a kindly woman who loved to play the melodeon and sing 'Slievenamon' and 'The Three-Leaf Shamrock'.

Providing a living for a large family on a small holding would not have been easy at the turn of the twentieth century, but the Quinns – like most of their kind – were hardworking, diligent and thrifty. Hugh Quinn was ploughing the land at the age of twelve and never really lost his love of the soil and of his homeplace. He nearly went to America when the threat of conscription loomed but (fortunately!) the immigration authorities closed off the route and he stayed on in Drumacon until the founding of the new state offered the opportunity to join An Garda Síochána. His parents were upset at the thought of losing their principal worker on the farm – he was also much-sought by neighbours who needed a helping hand at harvest time – but in truth there was plenty of help available by then. There was Jimmy, the quiet gentle bachelor who lived and worked all his long life in Drumacon. There was the jovial Charlie who was 'a terror for reading', wrote wonderful letters and told equally wonderful stories. Charlie would eventually marry and inherit the farm. Paddy – the youngest – was the only one to avail of a secondary education. He also joined the guards and later emigrated to America. There was the loving and wise Katie who loved school but was kept at home to help out in house and farm – as was the custom – and only married late in life. There was Susan, who was married and widowed within six years, remarried, became pregnant, developed appendicitis and died when doctors refused to operate on her. And there was my namesake – John – whom I absolutely adored.

When John was seven, a heavy stone crushed his foot. He spent months in hospital but – like his sister subsequently – was not treated properly. The foot decayed and became permanently deformed. His parents sent him away as a young man to learn the trade of saddlery and harness-making and he eventually set up his own business in a loft in Drumacon. To me as a young boy, a visit to Uncle John's loft was sheer bliss. Climbing the external stone stairway was an ascent into paradise. From the top of the stairs, Lake Muckno sparkled in the distance. Inside, Uncle John sat crouched over a last or wrestled with an enormous horse collar. Ranged all along the wall was a collection of strange and wonderful tools – hammers, awls, knives, pincers, lasts, lengths of waxen thread. On his workbench lay various works in progress – but overwhelming all else was the unmistakeable and forever delightful scent of leather. It wafted all about me and I willed it to enter every pore of my body. John was always so warm and welcoming to children, although he remained a bachelor all his life. He would produce 'the wee hammer' – one of his hammer repertoire which was ideal for a child – supply me with some leather off-cuts and a handful of brads (tiny nails) and I could spend a whole afternoon 'cobbling' at his bench. Uncle John became 'James' in my novel *Generations of the Moon* –

The loft was transformed into a workshop. Hughie and Pete built a workbench which ran the length of the room. James wrote to his former employer in Dublin and, within a week, a large consignment of leather, waxen thread, nails and various tools arrived at the railway station in Culloville. James was a very meticulous worker and arranged the tools and materials of his trade neatly around the room. Sarah loved to visit the loft, if only to inhale the comforting smell of leather and to marvel at the array of tools that hung on pegs along the wall. As James gradually picked up work, the number of visitors to the house grew and brought added interest to the life of the McKevitts. Although the customers gained access to the loft by an external stone staircase at the gable end of the house, their comings and goings were acutely observed by all of the family and were often the source of livelier than usual conversation over supper.

'Hasn't Barney McQuillan aged a terror?' Bridie would say. 'I didn't recognise him going up to the loft with the stoop that was on him.'

'He suffers a lot with his back,' James would explain.

'He suffers a lot with them six daughters of his, if ye ask me,' Hughie would add with a mischievous grin, 'every one of them lazier than the next' –

'And no oil paintings either!' Pete guffawed.

'Maybe one of you should take a daughter off Barney's hands,' Sarah suggested.

'Not if I was paid a king's ransom,' Hughie countered. 'Sure they'd scald you. Never do a hand's turn about the place! Isn't that what put their poor mother in an early grave – doing everything for them?'

'As long as they wear out their boots I'm happy,' James said with a quiet smile. And then they would move on to another visitor.

GENERATIONS OF THE MOON

Uncle John died rather suddenly after a bout of pneumonia in January 1955. It was my first experience of death in the family. I grieved for him greatly even though I was only thirteen years old. It was also my last winter in Ballivor. Soon we would move to Dublin. When my parents went to the funeral I looked after our little 'farm' at home, foddering the cattle, boiling up a big 'pig's pot' in the backyard and feeding the pigs. On my parents' return I was rewarded for my hard work with the gift of my first wristwatch. But without Uncle John and his magical leather-scented loft, Drumacon would never be the same again.

21 The Wee Hills II

Drumacon was Uncle John but it was also so much more. It was a range of innocent pleasurable pursuits – from the downright crazy and often painful 'roly-poly' (lying down at the top of a steep field and simply rolling all the way to the bottom) to exploring a hayloft or peering into the depths of a well or a dark flaxpool and wondering. Flax had been a valuable cash crop among the wee hills in the first half of the twentieth century. It was no longer harvested in my childhood but the dark pools remained and Aunt Katie's memories helped me fictionalise the flax-harvesting –

> *Blue. She remembered the blue of the flax in flower.*
> *People going the road would stop to look at it in the long*
> *field. It was a breathtaking sight. The blue faded. She was*
> *still looking down the long field. Fifteen men were ranged*
> *across its width, bent to the task of pulling the flax on a*
> *sultry August day. They would start at the far end and*
> *work their way towards the headland. They worked hard*
> *amid banter and laughter about football and girls and the*
> *gossip of the day. And always Pete edged ahead of the*
> *others. Hardly eighteen and stripped to the waist, his*
> *lithe bronzed body bent and rose to the task in an easy*
> *rhythm. And though they would jest and tease – 'God,*
> *Pete must have a woman waitin' for him at the*
> *headland', 'He'll not leave a heel of bread for us' –*

nobody could get ahead of him. He would give a little whoop when he reached the headland where Bridie and Sarah were waiting with cans of tea or buttermilk, great slabs of buttered slices of brown bread wrapped in newspaper and a bucket of hardboiled eggs. The men sat along the headland and ate and drank with relish as they eyed their morning's work with satisfaction. Occasionally someone would give a snatch of a song or a verse of a poem learned at school.

'Many's the time Master Connolly reddened me hands for not knowin' that oul' poem!'

'Ach, he wasn't the worst!'

'He was a cranky oul' get and no mistake! If I had him here now I'd feck him into that flaxpool!'

Laughter. Always laughter. And always the loudest laughter came from Pete McKevitt and Jimmy McCabe.

GENERATIONS OF THE MOON

There were other reminders of a past age. On the way to the house we passed by the 'dancing flags' where people would come 'from as far away as Blayney' for an evening's dancing by the roadside. The fire in the kitchen was kept alive by a bellows. We children craved a turn at the bellows wheel when the porridge pot was put on late at night. The adults each had a bowl of steaming porridge before retiring for the night. Once my father caught an eel in the river, sliced it up and fried it on the pan. I watched, fascinated and frightened, as the eel segments twisted and squirmed on the sizzling pan. Living so near to the border meant there was access to goods that were not available in 'the Free State'. A trip to Monaghan would always ensure a good stock of 'Tate and Lyle's Golden Syrup' to be brought home to Ballivor. Could there be any greater luxury than plastering your bread and butter liberally with Golden Syrup?

A trip to Michael Deery's Emporium in Carrickmacross was another source of wonder and delight, not so much for the fascination of 'departments' – such as Haberdashery, Millinery, Lingerie – as for the method of payment. The shop assistant would enclose the money tendered with the bill in a container which was then dispatched by means of a pulley system to a mysterious room that seemed to be suspended from the roof of the shop. Within minutes the container returned at great speed. The assistant opened it and handed you your bill and your change. I walked backwards out of Deery's, gazing open-mouthed at the room in the roof and wondered what went on up there.

Whether it was helping Aunt Katie find a hen who was 'laying out' in the hedge, or playing an interminable game of hurling with my brother in the haggard where two haystacks served as giant goal posts, Drumacon was always a delight. That delight was augmented by the landscape that differed so much from the plains of Meath, by the freedom and quiet it afforded, but above all else by my uncles and aunts – beautiful, simple, kind, loving and quiet-spoken people who were unassuming and expected little from life and to whom I am so very deeply indebted for their love and nurture.

22 Kildalkey

There is no saying that I can recall about Kildalkey. If there was, it would probably be 'Kildalkey, I hardly knew ye'. Although it was only four miles down the road from Ballivor, it was an even quieter and smaller village and we would have few reasons to go there. *Cill Dealga* – the church of *Dealga* – although it is more associated with St Dympna, whose holy well is said to have curative powers.

Ecclesiastically, Kildalkey was a separate parish, but in terms of civil jurisdiction it came under my father's beat. Hence his little black book also recorded 'found on the premises in Charlie Miggin's pub'; 'ragwort, thistle and dock rampant in Corballis'; and endless unlighted bikes from Frayne to Ballinadrimna. Kildalkey was hurling country so there would be occasional trips to a match there. Around 1950 the 'New Hall' was opened – it was part of the old Alms House – so there would be occasional concerts and variety shows for our entertainment. There was also the 'Silver Circle' – a weekly wheel-of-fortune which offered 'fantastic prizes' (£5? £1?) to those who entered the draw. Kildalkey was also horse country – Dick McCormack and Charlie Wellesley trained racehorses locally. And Kildalkey – or to be more precise, Rathcormack – was the home of the Potterton family of auctioneering fame ('T.E. [Potterton] will take care of all', the saying had it). The lives of the Potterton dynasty are recorded in that beautiful book *Rathcormack* by Homan Potterton, former director of the National Gallery in Dublin.

Our main reason for visiting Kildalkey, however, was to see another Potterton family, who were no relation to the Rathcormack dynasty. Tom and Rose (or 'Dodie', as she was affectionately called) Potterton lived in a cosy tin-roofed house (now demolished) that faced down the main street. They were a gentle and welcoming couple who had no children, but they had a sheepdog – Roy – who seemed almost human. According to Tom, Roy always knew when my father was approaching. He might be half a mile down the road when Roy's tail would start slapping against the floor. 'You'd better put on the kettle, Dodie,' Tom would say. 'The sergeant is coming!' The kettle would be boiled and a sweet treat produced for us children. I remember coming across a book in that house – a book by an author with a strange name – Hilaire Belloc.

When my brother Noel made his Confirmation, there was a surprise present from the Pottertons. The postman reached into his mailbag and produced a ball of fluff – a sheepdog pup. He was our first and only dog. (We had little luck with pets. Cat after cat mysteriously died. I remember digging up one cat grave in the long garden and being disappointed to discover that he hadn't gone to cat heaven. Finally we discovered TIBS cat powders and our first surviving cat was named after it.) Needless to say, our first dog was called Roy, after a very special dog who could always tell when the sergeant was coming …

Roy was later involved in a little incident that – while trivial – nonetheless indicates how almost static the pace of life was in the 1950s. I come home from school for my dinner. My father is talking with Jim Dargan, who is standing by his horse and cart in the middle of the street. What neither man notice is that the Clydesdale's mighty hoof is pinning the unfortunate Roy's paw to the road. Amazingly, the dog was uncomplaining until I released him, whereupon he whimpered away with a squashed paw. Trivial, yes. But to me it captures the almost undisturbed pace of a sleepy midlands village perfectly.

23 Football

For down here in Ballivor
We have fifteen gallant youths
Who don their colours white and red
And fifteen pairs of boots ...

THE BALLIVOR FOOTBALL SONG

The main sporting interests in the Ballivor of the 1940s and 1950s were football, football and football! Hurling was pursued on either side of us in Killyon and Kildalkey but Ballivor was football territory. The exploits of Ballivor teams are well documented in the ballads of Tom Kiernan (see *The Balladeer*). For the most part they languished in the intermediate ranks but victory over Trim in the Intermediate Championship Final of 1948 was a major breakthrough. This was a formidable outfit in the no-nonsense roughhouse style of the day. It was close-marking ('every man a man!'), get-there-first ('face the ball, lads'), catch-the-ball-and-belt-it-as-far-as-you-can stuff. And take no prisoners! When you were 'tackled' by Stonewall Dixon, Black Doyle or Pop Burke, you knew all about it.

It wasn't all muscle of course. We did have stylists like Jim Dargan (almost dainty in his movements) and Paud Conway (who would smooth back his hair before taking a free). As youngsters we would watch our heroes 'training' of a summer evening. 'Training' was simply a muster of whoever was

available for a kickabout. We would stand in the goalmouth –
or preferably well behind the goals – and call out to them in
Micheál O'Hehir parlance –

Send in a ground duster!
Make it a skyscraper!
Give us a piledriver!
One of your long ones!

– the latter, because, in truth, there was no joy in facing up to a
Dargan piledriver. If you were 'lucky' enough to stop it, your
hands stung for the rest of the evening.

No matter at what level a club operated, competition was
intense and there were many keen local rivalries. Ballinabrackey
from the Meath–Offaly border – or 'the Barmbracks' as we
called them – were particularly bitter rivals. Beating Trim in the
Intermediate Final was particularly sweet for Ballivor but it left
a sour taste with Trim, who suspected that Ballivor had used an
illegal player (Andy Clarke of the double name – see *The
Ballivor Football Song*) and objected – but Ballivor kept the
title. On the day Trim were very upset and 'Boiler' McGuinness
– the referee – had to be escorted home!

A year later, in 1949, 'Stonewall' Dixon brought further
honours to the village when he helped Meath win their first All-
Ireland Senior Football title. As a ballad of the time put it, 'he
bottled up Mick Higgins' and would have been a strong
contender for 'man of the match'. Ballivor had further success
in 1950 when they beat Donoughmore in the prestigious Feis
Cup Final (again, see *The Balladeer*). Almost fifty years later,
Paddy Dixon recalled a sweet personal memory with perfect
clarity –

I played the best I could but I hadn't scored right up until
the last minute. We were awarded a free and I took it. I
hit it so hard that my knee went up and hit my chin. I
nearly broke my own jaw! The ball sailed over the bar

and it banged up on the bank at the hospital end in Páirc Tailteann. It was the old heavy leather ball but I was a strong lad. She travelled low, climbing all the time like a jet leaving Collinstown! M.J. McGearty described it as 'a breathtaking point' in his match report. The final whistle went and we had won. Fr Tully, the County Board chairman, walked to where I had taken the free and put down a cigarette box as a marker. He called me over and we paced out the distance to the fifty-yard line. Thirty-five yards. Add on the fifty and that's eighty-five yards. And the ball must have gone another fifty yards onto the bank! Fr Tully said it was surely the longest free kick ever seen in Navan!

Another Ballivor man, Patsy McGearty, was 'between the sticks' for Meath when they won their second All-Ireland title in 1954, but for the 'red and whites' of Ballivor there would be lean pickings until they once again won the Intermediate Championship in 1971. In between, Meath had won a third All-Ireland title in 1967 and once again Ballivor contributed a 'stonewall' centre-half-back in Bertie Cunningham. The same Bertie had – as a strapping big *gossoon* – helped Ballivor win back-to-back Under-14 titles in 1952 and 1953. My brother Noel featured on those teams but missed out on his second medal. After much agitation he got that medal – fifty years later when the Under-14s celebrated the golden jubilee of their win!

Football is a serious business in Ballivor – and at the heart of that business over a long lifetime has been M.J. McGearty as trainer, secretary, keeper of the records and general motivator. Ballivor is very much in his debt.

> *So Ballivor dressed up in the white and the red*
> *With Dixon their captain right there at their head.*
> *He said 'Come on boys now, our bones will be sore*
> *Before we are finished with this Donoughmore'.*

24 1949 – Sam Arrives

And do you remember the September of '49
When we brought home 'Sam' for the very first time.
Oh, Cavan's Mick Higgins never tried his tricks on
When faced by our own 'Stonewall' Dixon ...
Oh goodnight Ballivor, I'll sleep in Trim.

It transpired that Ballivor's great local triumph at intermediate level in 1948 would only be a curtain raiser for the county's national victory the following year! Could we absorb it all? Yes, we could, but not without heart-stopping moments on the way – notably three great jousts with old rivals Louth! The force was with us and we eventually qualified to meet even deadlier rivals Cavan on that September afternoon in Croke Park. Cavan! We remembered with awe their great exploits two years previously in the Polo Grounds, New York. Cavan! The mention of individual names like Mick Higgins, Tony Tighe and the 'Gunner' Brady could strike fear into a young mind. But no, we had our heroes too – Paddy 'Hands' O'Brien, Christo Hand, Paddy Connell, Frankie Byrne, Paddy Meegan and the wonderfully wily 'Man in the Cap', Peter McDermott. And we had Ballivor's own Stonewall Dixon. Paddy Dixon had earned that *soubriquet* for being a classic old-style 'stopper' centre half-back. There was no way around him. When you ran into Paddy Dixon, you ran into a stone wall.

The 'hype' of modern All-Ireland finals was unknown in 1949 but we created our own innocent hype. I was a mere seven years old then, but I'm sure in endless backyard matches with my brother I 'pulled the ball out of the sky' *à la* Paddy O'Brien, 'floated over a delightful minor in the second moiety' (as the *Meath Chronicle* would put it) in the style of Frankie Byrne and made a tearful plea to the referee (our mother!) when my brother claimed a 'square ball' infringement as I fisted a Peter McDermott special to the net at the turf-shed goal. I like to think too that during that summer of '49 I took time out from playing in hayfields or on turfbanks to listen with serious intent to grown men's talk as they worked and rested.`

> *Dixon'll not let him away with much ...*
> *If Frankie has his shooting boots on ...*
> *A fellow from Skryne told me O'Brien has a bad leg.*
>   *I don't know for sure but that's what he told me ...*

And then the great day. Fr Farrell would have been too austere a man to pray for a Meath victory at Sunday Mass but in our hearts we prayed and hoped. The cars bearing those supporters lucky enough to attend (no worry about tickets in those days – you just went!) were cheered from the village. Would we be cheering them home in triumph that evening? The day dragged on. No *Sunday Game Live* then – but we had the vivid radio pictures painted by Micheál O'Hehir's commentary –

> *'I didn't hold him,' says Peter McDermott. 'You did hold him,' says referee Dan Ryan and Cavan's Paddy Smith takes the free. The ball comes dropping, dropping, dropping into the Meath goalmouth but Paddy Dixon, playing the game of his life, comes away with the ball ...*

Gathered around the Pye radio in the kitchen, we cheered our heroes' efforts to the echo. Our confidence grew as Meath edged ahead and stayed ahead! And then the sweetest words of all from Micheál O'Hehir –

There goes the final whistle and Meath are All-Ireland
Football Champions for the very first time …

Bedlam! We poured out into the village street, cheering and
dancing and trying to absorb the import of what we had just
heard. Meath. All-Ireland Senior Football Champions. We had
never heard those words before. The day would be etched in
our collective memory forever more. Nearly fifty years later
Paddy Dixon would recall his personal memory of the game
with the clarity and enthusiasm of a young man who had just
played 'the game of his life' –

> *It was a do-or-die effort – we were only two points in*
> *front. The Gunner Brady and me went for a ball. It should*
> *have been his ball – it was running to him. I saw him*
> *change his set coming to me and I said I was either going*
> *to break my neck or block him from kicking. He suddenly*
> *backed up and I had no option. I couldn't dip because if I*
> *dipped he'd have killed me. I drew my foot like that and*
> *didn't he draw late and hit me in the back … I spun round*
> *and round and I remember seeing the gutters on the old*
> *Hogan Stand twice! When I hit the ground on my third*
> *spin I saw stars and moons leppin' out of my head! I was*
> *nearly dead. Micheál O'Hehir said it was the shockingest*
> *crash that ever was heard in Croke Park. 'Dixon has to be*
> *dead!' he said, but I leaped up straight away. I was barely*
> *able to carry myself across the field but I kept hopping.*
> *My leg was that swollen that the next morning in Barry's*
> *Hotel I barely managed to get on the trousers of the new*
> *suit my poor mother had bought for me. But I wasn't*
> *worried about the swollen leg. We were heading for*
> *Navan that night with the Sam Maguire Cup …*

The excitement rose as the cars began to return to Ballivor on
the Sunday evening. Personal accounts were sought from those
who were fortunate enough to witness history in the making.

How did Dixon play?
Sure he bottled up Mick Higgins! Never gave him a smell
of the ball …

As the September dusk descended, it was time to light the bonfire. Sergeant Quinn would never know that his sons colluded with others in 'borrowing' hay and turf from the barn at the rear of the barracks in order to get the fire going.

Improvisation became the order of the evening. Blazing sods of turf perched precariously on long forked sticks generated a torchlight procession down the main street in the gathering gloom – chanting, cheering, crazy. The master of improvisation was Joe Dempsey, our very own Micheál O'Hehir impressionist. We gathered around the bonfire as Joe 'replayed' the game (our *Sunday Game!*) from the pre-match parade to the very last kick of the ball, incorporating every catchphrase and cliché from the master's voice. We cheered every Meath score, hailed every Dixon clearance, lustily and roundly booed every Cavan foul and score.

In the crowded bars of McLaughlin's, Kelly's and Walsh's pubs, our elders analysed the game in their own particular wisdom but as the bonfire sparks rocketed into the night sky (*Go on – get another armful of turf – he won't mind!*) we were sated by Joe Dempsey's gradual crescendo to that wondrous climax. Then back down the street and into Pat McGearty's house to hear stories of daring deeds of yesteryear.

Ba lá dár saol é – it was a day of our lives, never to be recaptured. There would be other great days with Ballivor involvement – Patsy McGearty in 1954, Bertie Cunningham (another Stonewall!) in 1967, Conor Martin in 1996 – but there never would be a day like that September Sunday in 1949. Twenty years later man would walk on the moon, but on that glorious, crazy, turf-blazing night in a Meath village, a seven-year-old boy had already been over that moon, round it and back again. Sixty years later he delights in cartwheeling through the memory of it all.

25 The Man in the Cap

We called him The Higgler – he sold eggs by the dozen
In his shop he treated you like the Pope was your cousin
But when he played football we cheered and we clapped
And we simply called him – The Man in the Cap.

When Sam Maguire first came to Meath
We had fifteen heroes out on that field
O'Brien and Dixon were manning the gap
And leading up front was – The Man in the Cap.

Fast forward now to '54
And Sam Maguire comes home once more
Who drove home in his Hillman with the cup in his lap?
Our very own captain – The Man in the Cap.

In '68, Meath blazed a trail down under
When Cunningham and Collier tore the Galahs asunder
And who had the Aussies in such a flap?
The Royal's manager – The Man in the Cap.

You can have Maradona and his Hand of God
You can even give Georgie Best the nod
Throw in David Beckham – and Posh the bould strap!
I'd swap them all for – The Man in the Cap.

When Meathmen gather to discuss the greats
They're more poetic than Heaney or Yeats
And who's their favourite? Who is their Nap?
You've guessed it, my friends – it's The Man in the Cap.

So come my friends and let's raise a toast
To the man whose achievements we all boast
A right royal sportsman – a wonderful chap
Let's raise the rafters for The Man in the Cap.

Written to mark the civic reception given by Meath County Council on 19 April 2007 to honour the great Peter McDermott – 'The Man in the Cap', and my childhood hero.

26   The Farm

My father loved to say, 'You can take the man from the bog, but you can never take the bog from the man'. If that is true, then it is equally true with regard to the land in the case of my father. An Garda Síochána may have taken him from the land but it never took the land from him. He had served a tough apprenticeship on the home farm among the wee hills of Monaghan, ploughing the 'stony grey soil' at twelve years of age. When he settled in Ballivor as Garda Sergeant he became as much a farmer – or at least a self-sufficient provider – as an upholder of the law.

It was very much a culture of the time – mid-1930s onwards – to be self-sufficient. Eamon de Valera promoted it as Taoiseach. There was ample time available for my father. He had the assistance of four gardaí in upholding the law, at a time when 'unlighted bikes were the greatest sin'. I can very much empathise with John McGahern when he recalls the 'patrol accounts' written up by the gardaí who served under his father in Cootehall, Co. Leitrim –

> Most of the accounts that were written into the big ledgers, in good weather and in bad, were fictitious, and were referred to laughingly as Patrols of the Imagination, but never by my father. Many of the patrols they cycled out on were spent working in their gardens of conacre or on their plots of turf on Gloria Bog. Only when the

monthly inspection from the superintendent was due or a surprise inspection feared were the patrols observed and reported properly. Even then some invention was probably needed, as hardly anything ever happened on those potholed roads ...

I suspect that Ballivor was little different from Cootehall in the matter of police patrols.

All this apart, my father engaged in 'farming' probably because he simply loved it. It was the life he had grown up with. In truth he probably looked on himself as a farmer who was a part-time guard rather than the other way around. To me he always seemed happiest when working the soil, humming 'South of the Border' as he scattered dung, or a Delia Murphy favourite as he snagged turnips. He tilled every inch of the substantial barrack garden, borrowing a horse and plough to break the soil and open drills (a simple task compared to dealing with the contours of a Monaghan hill), so that visitors to the barracks made their way up the avenue through a forest of potatoes on one side and a sea of turnips on the other. At least they seemed like forest and sea to my childhood eye, as I served my apprenticeship in scattering dung or dropping seed potatoes. He was a meticulous worker, all the time telling me to 'take it cushy' – something he rarely did himself.

Surprisingly, he never tilled the long garden behind our house but he regularly took conacre for hay or other fodder crops. I remember a thoroughly miserable wet day when my brother and I were kept home from school (hooray!) to thin an enormous (to us) field of turnips (boo!). My mother came too and we toiled up and down sodden drills on sack-wrapped knees. Within an hour Master Conway's algebraic equations began to appear more enticing than yet another drill of stubborn and slippery turnip plants. Conacre was also taken for hay and again as children we were pressed into service for turning the drying hay (a tedious process) and for cocking the hay (an art in itself to complete a symmetrical and weatherproof structure). The rewards were the many jaunts up and down the village from the meadow to the barracks haybarn on the horse-drawn hay bogey. I have a warm memory of village children clambering aboard the empty bogey on the outward journey (pity the poor horse!). In the meadow, the haycock was magically winched aboard the canted bogey and I rode home in style up front with my father – to the envy of my village friends.

It is still a mystery to me how my father appropriated the barrack outbuildings for his own farming purposes. Maybe he paid a rent but, whether or which, those buildings housed two cows, a calf or two, winter fodder, and – as mentioned earlier – an unused room in the barrack itself was devoted to sprouting seed potatoes.

Of course ours wasn't 'a farm' but it had all the elements of a full-scale operation and for a young boy it offered an agricultural education in miniature. Digging into a frosted pit of mangolds before pulping them manually in the Pierce pulper. Feeding the pulp and hay to the cows in their stalls, gladly absorbing the heat of their bodies. Learning to milk the cows, cleaning out their stalls and later scattering the dung along the potato drills. All of this was a practical education. Not to mention bringing a cow to the bull down in Crossanstown and being exposed to the mystery of raw sex (needless to say, the only sex education I ever received!). Later I would assist in and witness the miraculous birth of a calf, hauled from its groaning mother's womb by a rope tied to its hooves. Life and growth and renewal were all about me.

And death also. In our own backyard we kept pigs and turkeys. One of my duties was to boil the 'pig's pot' – a half-barrel of potatoes cooked over an open fire in the yard. It was the preparation that I dreaded, especially in winter. The potatoes first had to be washed in icy water. I wince now at the memory of plunging my chilblained hands into that freezing water to loosen the mud from those potatoes. Only when I got a roaring fire going did sensation return to my fingers.

Despite that, I have always liked pigs. In my radio days I made a documentary entitled *Pighomage* – a celebration of the pig, to make up for the bad press he invariably gets. Once I was present for the killing of a pig. It is a searing, jumbled memory of terrifying ear-splitting screams, basins of hot water, startling red free-flowing blood, pink quivering flesh, strange knotted innards, a milky-coloured bladder that would become a football, empty eyes staring out at me. Once. Enough for evermore.

And then there were the turkeys. My mother's province. They came as 'day-old chicks' in ventilated boxes on the Ballina bus. She would feed them a mixture of hardboiled eggs and nettles (ouch!) and let them run free in the long garden for their short lives. (Once – on the advice of a friend – there was an experiment with guinea hens. A total disaster. Unlike their domesticated turkey cousins, these wild creatures were uncontrollable. They would take flight from our yard, swoop across the street – narrowly missing the bus from Ballina – and proceed to roost in the trees in the grounds of the Protestant church – the shame of it! – or on the roof of Garda Maguire's house. We would spend hours trying to coax them down and round them up. Never again, my mother swore.)

Early in December there was more slaughter, probably with the help of the butcher across the street. Necks were methodically wrung, and on the 8th of December the lifeless birds were stuffed into the boot of the Baby Ford (AI 4872) – or later the Ford Prefect (AI 9052) – to accompany the family on the Christmas expedition to Dublin. The turkeys were sold to Carton Bros., Poultry Merchants, Cabra. On then to the city centre where my father would park outside Clerys and we would all enter that wonderful department store and complete our shopping in one location. No doubt distractions were provided for the children so that mother could have the opportunity to shop for Santa Claus. For me there was distraction enough in the fascinating pneumatic chute at each counter through which payment and bill were dispatched, to return magically moments later with receipt and change. Another welcome distraction would be a meal in the restaurant – a rare treat – before the climax of the day and the ultimate treat – a visit to the cavernous Theatre Royal for a variety show. Echoing in the recesses of my mind is the gravelly voice of Noel Purcell singing –

You push the poker in and you pull the poker out
And the smoke goes up the chim-a-nee all the time

Oh happy day ...

No, the barrack garden wasn't a farm, but it was a beautiful experience of the soil and the animal world. And a lasting experience. Nearly six decades later, if I haven't got my early potatoes planted before St Patrick's Day, I hear my father's voice gently chiding me. And yet if I set to opening drills at a furious pace to make up for lost time, he is there again, telling me to 'take it cushy now ...'

27 Trim

O goodnight Ballivor, I'll sleep in Trim ...

And what was Trim anyway? Trim was El Dorado, the Golden City, the seat of all worldly pleasures. Although it was only nine miles away from Ballivor, a visit to Trim was a rare enough treat. Some of the visits were functional – a trip to Jimmy Dunne, the barber, to McConville's Drapery for new clothes or to 'Mac's' shoe store. The McGonagles who owned 'Mac's' were family friends. A visit there meant the added treat of a 'high tea'. The children would play and explore the busy shoe-repair business 'out the back' while the adults talked – until Mrs McGonagle summoned us to the largesse of her dining table.

'Kneel up there, gossoon, like a good man!' Jimmy Dunne would bark before setting to my curling locks with his snapping scissors. I gripped the headrest of his big chair and winced as the gleaming scissors nipped around my ears. The men talked about football, horses and women but I closed my eyes and dreamed of my eventual escape with a shilling in my fist to Moore's Newsagents. Moore's was Utopia – the home of the *Beano*, the *Dandy* and my own favourite comic – *Radio Fun*, which featured 'The Falcon – police can't catch him; all crooks fear him!', and 'Inspector Stanley, the man with a thousand secrets'. The shilling grew clammy in my hand – decisions would have to be made and I would have to have enough money left over for a roll of caps for my six-shooter. There were a number of outlaws to be rounded up before the streets of Ballivor were safe again. A quick dash to The Bon-Bon, where there was a bewildering array of sweets and ice-creams to tantalise a young boy. Banana Whirls, bullseyes, fizz-bags, Yorkshire Toffees, liquorice sticks ... oh Trim, you stole my heart and my shilling away.

Not all trips to Trim were functional. There might be a play or musical show staged by the Dramatic Society in the Town Hall. An important hurling or football match in the GAA pitch. There were the delights of the pictures, and the ultimate in cinematic luxury was the occasional trip to the Royal Cinema in Trim. To be summoned on a Sunday evening with the words 'We're going to the pictures!' was a cause of utter delight. Here was regal treatment indeed – plush red seats (preferably on the balcony), a shop offering sweets and ice-cream, the welcoming sound of 'The Cuckoo Waltz'. The lights are dimmed, the music fades. A hush of anticipation as the curtains draw back to reveal a 'full supporting programme'. Pathe News, a Joe McDoaks 'funny', a cartoon, a John A. Fitzpatrick travelogue ('And so we say farewell to this exotic island ...'), a trailer for next week and then – THE BIG PICTURE! Please let it not be what my father called 'an ould woman's picture'. Edward G. Robinson hopefully, as 'Little Caesar'. Afterwards there would be supper in McGonagle's house before we set off home with the family rosary vying for attention with memories of *Little Caesar*.

> *Take that, you no-good cop! ...*
> *The Fifth Glorious Mystery – the Coronation of Our*
> *Blessed Lady ...*
> *It's no use, Rico. We've got you surrounded. Come on*
> *out!*
> *Your Decade! ...*

The house where I was born ...

Hugh and Bridget Quinn
Wedding Photograph, 1931

John Quinn, Confirmation Day
4 May 1954

*My father (left) in his early days
in An Garda Sịochána*

*Charles & Katie Quinn
Drumacon*

Main Street, Ballivor, 1932

Around the Fire, Ballivor 1954,
Self, Mother and Noel

Drumacon
Defending the haystack goal!

The smile that welcomed most of
us into the world, Elizabeth Hiney

Senior Pupils, Ballivor NS 1954 – Author, 3rd from right, 2nd row

St Kinneth's
Church of Ireland

'Cinema Paradiso'... Sherrock's
garage today, its glory days gone

The author
at the village pump!

Ballivor...
the centre of the universe!

Johnny Kelly
April 1994

Recording 'A Day on the Bog'
19 July 1996

The Heroes of 1948: Ballivor – Meath Intermediate Football Champions
Back: C. McGarry, Chairman, M. Kiernan, Hon. Sec., M.J. McGearty, J. McGearty, P. Dixon,
P. Conway, P. McGearty, A. Rispin, W. Dixon, P. Burke, Rev. T. Dowling,
Middle: T. Daly, J. Dargan, M. Reilly, T. Doyle, Cap., P. Rispin, M. Dempsey, J. Doyle,
Front: K. Rispin, T. Regan.

Frank Dempsey on his last day as postman
(Hugh Gunn's Pharmacy (yellow) in rear)

Modern Ballivor
(Taken from almost the same position as the Frank Dempsey photo above)

Trim was the majesty of King John's castle and the sweep of the
historic river Boyne, but it was also the unspoken fear of the
County Home, where many of the old and feeble would end
their days. It is suggested that it was the refuge of the County
Home that our drunken friend had in mind when he uttered
those immortal words – 'Goodnight, Ballivor, I'll sleep in Trim'.

28 The Unusual

Yes – I suppose by today's criteria it was a boring life. Predictable, restricted, confined – all those things – but boring was never in our vocabulary. And there were unusual and exceptional events – like the day the aeroplane came.

I like to think I led the charge from the school playground when the plane landed in the cowplot across the road. It had come from Weston aerodrome in Dublin and, no, it wasn't in difficulty. It was a promotional stunt to advertise the fact that on the following Sunday a six-seater plane would come to take us on an aerial tour of Ballivor. A windsock was erected and the six-seater duly landed among grass tufts and cowpats on the Sunday. My mother and I were among the volunteers who paid seven shillings and sixpence for the thrill of being squeezed into a tiny cabin and taken on a twenty minute trip. The memory of it is vague but the overriding emotion was probably one of terror – and anxiety about landing safely! But we were in an aeroplane for the first time – and we survived.

Horse events dominated our calendar. The annual Gymkhana was held each August in Bracken's Field – a colourful assembly of horse races, novelty games, hawkers, ballad sellers and trick-o-the-loops (notably the three-card trickster). The races were short events where the horses had to circle a pole before returning to the starting point. Paddy Cunningham would bellow on the megaphone: 'Would competitors for the next race come to the start *immediately*!'

and for successive years the Gymkhana was dominated by an amazing little pony called Hello Paddy.

The Tara Harriers Annual Point-to-Point was held in Dalystown, near Trim. For us it was a day off school. This was more serious stuff. We assembled on a central hill to watch the progress of lengthy steeplechases through ploughed fields and pastures, over ditches and logs, now disappearing from view and finally surging up the finishing straight to raucous cheers. Bookmakers attended the Point-to-Point, so there was money to be made and lost.

The English Grand National was always followed avidly in the village. A trusted local man would gather our wagers and place them with a bookmaker in Trim, while we gathered around the wireless to hear Micheál O'Hehir, Peter O'Sullevan and others relay the fate of our collective shillings each way. My father always consulted the *Mutt and Jeff* cartoon in the newspaper on the night before the Big Race, convinced that there was a tip for the race secreted somewhere in Mutt and Jeff's doings. It never occurred to him that a US-originated syndicated cartoon could hardly be expected to forecast the winner of a race in England. No. There was a tip in there, somewhere. The trick was to find it.

On Easter Monday, the Black Maria came around to collect gardaí who would be on duty at Fairyhouse Races. For me the attraction of this day was the opportunity to collect car numbers ... I sat on the path outside our house and noted in a copybook the registration numbers of the passing cars. Variety was all-important. BI was Monaghan, EI was Sligo, NI was Wicklow, LI was Westmeath. Being the sergeant's son gave me the inside track on all this information. Not the most exciting of pursuits, but it passed a couple of hours. Look, there's a DI – that's Roscommon.

Apart from the regular trips to Trim, the summer trips to Monaghan and the annual trip to Dublin, my world was a very prescribed and local one. There were occasional sallies into other worlds. Barney Eivers – the local vet – would bring me on his 'house calls' now and then to places like Summerhill or Longwood and introduce me to the world of animal illness. I was intrigued by the very titles of their complaints, never mind their symptoms or treatment – timbertongue, red murrain and lockjaw. Again, a Bord na Móna driver would bring me for Saturday trips in his lorry to exotic places like Rhode or Clonsast in Co. Offaly, buy me a toffee bar and sing 'On Top of Old Smokey' mightily as we careered down dusty bog roads. There was no talk of insurance or the dangers of abuse. These were simply adults who had time for children and were friendly, interesting and interested in a child's life.

A family trip to Mullingar was rare but rich in promise. We were friendly with the Broder family who owned a hotel in the town, so a visit there guaranteed the mother of all mixed grills!

During my last summer in Ballivor I got a little taste of independence when my parents allowed me to spend a day in Dublin in the company of a new friend – Camillus Maye. The Mayes had moved to Ballivor from Dublin, so Camillus was deemed to be streetwise enough to escort me to the city. Off we went on the morning bus and in a crammed and exciting day (during which no doubt my mother said several rosaries for my safe return) we fitted in a visit to the Corinthian cinema (for a 3-D spectacular where tomahawks came hurtling out of the screen at us), Hector Grey's Emporium of Wonders (where I bought a toy projector which showed tiny cartoons on the wall) and several other bargain bazaars that only a native of the city could know and find in one day. We duly arrived home safely on the evening bus, laden with trinkets and playthings, among which was my first ever record purchase – a '45' of 'Oh Mein Papa' played by Eddie Calvert and his Golden Trumpet. 'What is the world coming to at all, at all?' I could hear *mein papa* say.

29 The Coming of the Light

It surprises me now to be reminded that the electric light did not come to Ballivor until the autumn of 1954 – at which time I was away in boarding school. The Rural Electrification Scheme was a massive undertaking for the ESB and when the 'wiremen' moved into an area they caused no little curiosity and in some cases a good deal of suspicion. People who had lived their lives by the light of candle, oil or 'tilly' lamp were naturally wary of this invisible power running through their houses. One way of persuading the doubters was to tell them that O'Hehir's GAA commentaries would in future 'only come out through the electric [radio] and not through the battery' ... Further, some of them resented their land being invaded by the wiremen. (*'The feckin' BSA are after puttin' up a pole in my field.'*)

Nevertheless, the coming of the wiremen added to the social and sporting life of the village for the best part of a year – and to its economic life also. My mother took in two lodgers – Barney McEneaney, the canvasser, and Angus Ryan, the engineer. Others who found lodgings were Pádraig McGinn, the clerical officer, and Tony Wilson, the mapman. The canvasser's job could be difficult – trying to enlist the doubters and the suspicious – but Barney McEneaney had a formidable ally in the parish priest, Fr Kiernan, who 'dealt with the "backsliders" on his own terms' (I am indebted to Pádraig McGinn for that quote). Fr Kiernan was a forceful man whom you didn't want to cross.

In his book *The Quiet Revolution – The Electrification of Rural Ireland*, Michael Shiel quotes from the Rural Area Engineer's final report from Ballivor in praise of Fr Kiernan:

> From the first day of arrival he gave the construction crew every assistance, got accommodation for them and, on the spiritual side, with the help of the Area Organiser Barney McEneaney, arranged a special retreat at times most suitable for their working hours. If we ever decide to have a patron priest of rural electrification, he is readymade!

Shiel further quotes from Noel McCabe, 'a veteran of those early days' –

> To ensure the maximum attendance, Fr Kiernan visited the local hostelries and 'requested' the owners to close down for an hour each evening while the retreat was in progress. However, being a just man, he also 'requested' the local Sergeant not to visit the pubs for a corresponding period after closing time!

I would be intrigued to learn if the very conscientious Sergeant acceded to the forceful parish priest's 'request'! We will never know.

Pádraig McGinn's memories of his time in Ballivor are interesting and insightful. The ESB gang arrived in Ballivor in February 1954. It was quite a change from their previous job in Rathfeigh Rural Area for which period they lodged in Drogheda. The Co. Louth town had 'two cinemas, coffee bars, a public library, a bookshop and a handball alley'. Ballivor, by contrast, 'looked miserable in the rain and slush of February – one street with a house or two boarded up and little sign of life. We used the upstairs room in one of those houses for an office'. Pádraig McGinn was a Castleblayney man. He did his best to integrate himself into the social life of the village and joined the football team.

'I played in a challenge game against Trim and used my speed to give a local butcher the runaround. A week or two later we played Navan O'Mahonys in the championship at Navan (travelling in the cab of a lorry with most of the team in the back ...) Within a minute of the start someone closed my right eye with a box in an off-the-ball incident ... I wanted to go off but our subs were poor and, foolishly, I was prevailed upon to stay on ...' Welcome to Meath football, Pádraig!

The wiremen also brought romance to the village, as Pádraig McGinn remembers.

Angus Ryan had an eye for the girls. Once he spotted Carmel Hiney down the village and wondered how he might make contact with her. I suggested he write a note to her, but he didn't want to do that in case he might be rebuffed. Tony Wilson and I volunteered to write the note so Angus could disclaim it if the plan misfired. After much hilarity, Tony and I composed the note in which Angus invited Carmel to the pictures in Trim that night. Tony was despatched to hand the note into Hineys' while Angus and I watched through the back window of the ESB van ... When Tony got to Hineys', Carmel's younger sister was standing at the door. Tony lost his nerve, kept going and bought three ice-cream cones in Murtagh's shop! We ate the ice-cream but Angus, being Tony's boss, ordered him to go back and deliver the note. He did and ten minutes later the sister dropped a reply into the ESB letterbox. The rest is history. Angus and Carmel were engaged some months later ...

Innocent times!

Pádraig McGinn bought a second-hand car in McEvoy's garage – 'a re-bored 1937 Model Y Ford, AI 5035' – even though he had very little driving experience. When Meath faced Cavan in Croke Park that summer, Pádraig intended going by bus, but Lily Brown – home on holiday from nursing in

England – persuaded him that 'there was nothing to driving'. 'I believed her and invited her to come with me. Meath won. When I tried to start the car to come home, it wouldn't start. Some Cavan supporters told us to sit in, turn on the ignition and put it in second gear. They started it with a push. On the way home I discovered that the brakes didn't work and later on that the wipers only worked when it wasn't raining or snowing …'

Welcome to Ballivor, Pádraig!

Despite these setbacks, Pádraig enjoyed his time in Ballivor, often playing cards at night in the Sergeant's house. 'Ballivor had its charms in summer and a walk along the Stoneyford river or down the quiet road towards the bog was peaceful and colourful with wild flowers, furze and hawthorn in bloom. Cars were few and the pace of life was slow …' Once the chemist, Hugh Gunn, took Pádraig fly-fishing and – to Hugh's disgust – Pádraig caught two fine trout using worms!

There was work to be done also, of course – and it was done quite efficiently. All summer long we children watched as great holes were dug in the village pathways, huge creosoted poles were erected and wiremen shimmied up the poles wearing crampons. Then the wires were pulled through and attached to the tops of the poles. We would parrot the wireman as he called out to his colleague down the street – 'Take up more slack … A bit more … Mark her off there … O.K.'

By the autumn the wiremen had moved to the Kildalkey area and by November they were moving on to Ballinagh in Co. Cavan. The initial wiring of a house was basic – one light, one switch, one plug per room – as electrical appliances were scarce enough at the beginning. When the electric light came on it showed up the housekeeping inadequacies ('Holy Mother of God, look at all the DUST!'). Managing the new power in the house required some adjustment. When Master Flood set an essay on 'The Electric Light', Paul Doyle wrote: 'It's a great yoke but when you get into bed you'd need a forty-foot pole to switch it off'! Much easier to snuff out a candle …

The street lighting made a total transformation in the village. How often had we negotiated our way down the street in pitch blackness, grateful for the occasional oil lamp in a window that lighted our way. Now all was changed. Our night town was ablaze every night. I missed the big switch-on (boarding school) but our football star Patsy McGearty remembers it clearly – 'It was the Wednesday night before the All-Ireland Football Final [where Meath would face and beat Kerry]. Paddy Dixon and I were coming home from training. We stopped at McKay's gate, confronted by an illuminated village street. "Jesus," said Dixon, "is the village on fire or what?"' When Christmas came, Patsy – with the help of Johnny Murtagh, Pierce Hiney and Johnny Corrigan (father of chef Richard) – erected Ballivor's first illuminated Christmas tree. They didn't bother with such details as planning permission. They just dug a hole in the path outside the church and plugged into the power in McGearty's house. It was a thing of rare beauty, festooned with cotton wool decorations and lights made of china. 'And do you know what?' says Patsy, 'it was the only illuminated Christmas tree between Dublin and Ballina …' Who am I to dispute that?

30 *Johnny*

Lines composed on the death of local hero Johnny Corrigan

You were a mighty man.
I gazed in childhood awe
At your manly frame
Crowned by those flowing locks.
You were lord of the dance
And of the playing fields,
Doughty half-back,
Fearless, regal in the air,
Deft wielder of the *camán*.

You knew too
The lure and the lore
Of bog pool and river,
Trapper of eels
And poacher of salmon.
You sowed and savoured
The fruits of rich bog earth.
The King of Robinstown!
How fitting that a piper
Should welcome you home
To Kilaconnigan
And to Glory.

JOHN QUINN
09.07.2003

138

The Germans are
31 Coming! The Germans
are Coming!

When Adolf Hitler began occupying small nations in 1939, a group of concerned citizens of Ballivor met to discuss how they might resist the threat of a Nazi invasion. One practical step taken was to erect tar barrels and wooden spikes in Walsh's Big Meadow to prevent the Luftwaffe landing there. And the name of the village was painted over on the school wall. In the event, only one German arrived …

A Sunday night in May 1940. Liam Murphy and his wife were cycling home from the pictures in Trim when they heard a plane circling overhead. M.J. McGearty had been at a play in Nixon's Garage (could it have been local dramatist Mick Kiernan's *Sugar for Jam*?) and was now tucked up in his bed when he heard the unusual noise in the distance. Over the next couple of days the aeroplane was the talk of the village. Inevitably, some people claimed they saw the German 'dropping from the sky' into an area known as 'The Currachs'.

The German was Herman Goerz and Kit Reilly came across him hiding in the bushes. 'Where am I?' Goerz enquired. Kit pointed out the spire of Ballivor church in the distance. 'That's Ballivor church,' said Kit. 'You're in Ballivor, that's where you are!'

Kit was rewarded for his kindness with a crisp ten shilling note, but his conscience must have troubled him because he reported the matter to Sergeant Quinn, who alerted the Army. By the Friday Ballivor was the scene of intense activity as the

Army patrolled every crossroads in the area. The Sergeant conducted his own investigation – with little enough success. One man refused him entry to his house on the grounds that he had a 'delicate' wife within ... Goerz was obviously assisted locally until he was spirited away after a week or so. He eventually made his way to Wicklow and remained on the run for ten months. He left a couple of souvenirs behind. One local man wore the German's frieze coat for years and even more astonishingly, many years later, Master Carey confiscated a 'toy gun' in the schoolyard. It was a tiny pistol that Goerz had left behind.

Goerz was eventually arrested in Wicklow, imprisoned and after the war was sentenced to deportation to Germany. He contested this decision in court, lost the case and – obviously fearful of what might befall him on his return home – he bit a 'button' from his jacket and swallowed it. It was a strychnine tablet. A sad and highly dramatic end to the German invasion of Ballivor. Herman Goerz is buried in the aliens' plot in Glencree cemetery in Co. Wicklow.

> *And once there came from out the sky*
> *A most mysterious German spy.*
> *He came not to plunder nor to pillage*
> *But said, on seeing our sleepy village,*
> *   O gute nacht, Ballivor. Ich will in Trim schlafen!*

32   Getting There

We were lucky in the Quinn household in that we always had a car at our disposal. My father had a car from the time he got married. My mother recalled their arriving in Ballivor from Co. Limerick in 1935 in 'a little Morris Cowley'. The first car I remember was a black 'Baby Ford' – AI 4872 – which was cramped enough when we all squeezed in for a trip to Monaghan or to the seaside at Bettystown or for that Christmas adventure in Dublin, but it was still luxury. Many families did not have a car. My father cherished his car, washing and waxing it often and keeping it regularly serviced in Mick Smyth's garage in Trim. You held your breath on frosty mornings when the 'choke' was fully extended and your father swung the starting handle – until finally the engine jumped to life with a judder. I clearly remember the excitement when my father arrived home unexpectedly in a gleaming new black (of course) Ford Prefect – AI 9052. We had come up in the world! And this state of the art model had to be driven carefully for the first few months while you were 'running in' the engine.

The bicycle was the ubiquitous mode of transport. To own a bicycle was a mark of distinction, especially if it was a stout Raleigh with a three-speed gear and a dynamo (no fear of Sergeant Quinn stopping you on a dark night!). I never had my own bicycle. I had to make do with my mother's machine but there was no shame in riding a lady's bike – apart from not being able to 'offer a crossbar' to your pals. The bicycle got you to football matches, to the river for a swim, to the bog, or to no place in particular when you just went cycling around for fun. For the grown-ups the bicycle brought them to the cinema in Trim or to a dancehall – when the ultimate male triumph would be to have his dance partner accept the offer of 'a crossbar home' with a possible dalliance on the way!

> *The crowd poured out into the welcome cool of a June night. There was excited chatter, whoops of laughter and the odd ribald comment as bicycles were retrieved from hedges. Inevitably the voice of Jimmy McCabe rose above all others – 'the only conveyance here with a padded crossbar. No, Canon. I'm sorry. It's reserved!' There was immediate uproarious laughter.*
>
> GENERATIONS OF THE MOON

I never rode my father's bike. It was a giant of a thing and had an air of authority and officialdom about it. After all, it was the Sergeant's bike – used in the relentless pursuit of unlighted cycles, straying animals and noxious weeds. For all that, I was intrigued to learn in recent years that the Sergeant had once loaned his bike to Johnny Kelly to attend a match in Navan (eighteen miles away). Johnny and a friend parked their bikes 'in the bushes' in the grounds of Navan hospital. Imagine their consternation on returning to find both bikes missing! Above all else, the *Sergeant's* bike was gone. Calamity of calamities! The two men searched desperately for an hour until a hospital groundsman summoned them to reveal the two bikes locked away in a shed! 'Don't ever damage my shrubs like that again!' he warned them.

There was public transport of course. The Dublin–Ballina bus stopped at Kelly's Greyhound Bar twice a day (travelling in both directions). And the Dublin–Sligo train could be boarded at the Hill of Down, five miles away. During the war years, travel was particularly difficult. Eithne Conway recalls how it took her two days to travel the seventy-five miles to boarding school in Monaghan – sidecar from Ballivor to the Hill of Down, train to Mullingar, change train for Cavan, spend the night in Cavan, train next morning to Clones and finally bus from Clones to Monaghan! Now *there* was dedication to education. Mickey Miggin ran a hackney car – usually for emergencies – and when it came to transporting the Ballivor football team to matches, most of them would pile into the back of an open lorry! The 'Barmbracks' invariably arrived from Ballinabrackey in a *bus*! Show-offs!

If all else failed, of course, you walked. People used Shank's mare quite a bit and I suppose we were all the healthier for it. Still, nothing could beat the exhilaration of flying along the open and traffic-free road on your bicycle. Struggle to the top of the rise, then slip her into top speed and tear downhill. Made it ma, as Jimmy Cagney would say. Top of the world!

33 The Forge

In his forge, the genial blacksmith Bill Kelly
Crouched beneath a horse's belly
And there, amid smut and steam and sparks and smoke
He hammered and turned and shaped – a joke.

Bill Kelly's forge stood behind Murtagh's shop at the bottom of the street. It was a dark and daunting place to enter – save when a blast of the bellows suddenly breathed life into the fire on the raised altar in the centre of the building. The red and orange glow banished the gloom and revealed strange shapes silhouetted in the inner recess against a shower of sparks. A centaur? No, merely Bill grappling with a huge Clydesdale as he filed down a hoof before fitting a shoe on the restive animal.

The place may have been daunting but its owner was always welcoming. He had an easy, jovial manner, a man who liked to share funny stories and jokes. A prankster too. Was he not one of the 'welcoming party' who greeted Nancy and John Murtagh on their return from their honeymoon? Nancy was remarrying as a widow and there seemed to be a ritual of welcoming such couples by hooting through improvised bugles (often broken bottles). A similar party waited for the newly-weds Nanto and Tommy Ryan at Davis's Corner but the Ryans were tipped off and made their way quietly to Muchwood by a back road ...

The bellows gives an asthmatic wheeze. The orange glow illuminates the forge. Bill Kelly pokes through the red embers, sending a shower of smuts across the room. He eventually withdraws an incandescent horseshoe from the fire and briefly holds it aloft before laying it on the anvil. He proceeds to hammer and twist the shoe into the exact required shape. Sparks flit past his crouched form. He plunges the shoe into a barrel of water. Steam now joins the smut and smoke, causing my eyes to smart, parching my nose and throat. The increasingly acrid smells drive me to the door, but before I escape I must witness the final act of the smith's performance. He turns his back on the Clydesdale, draws the hairy hoof between his knees, measures shoe to hoof and affixes it by driving home a series of glistening tapered nails into the massive hoof. I wince at the thought of nails entering flesh, but of course they don't and the horse stands impassive on three legs.

'Are you off so?' Bill calls.

I nod, blinking the soot from my eyes.

'I'll see you tomorrow then. Give you another crack at the title!' he chortles.

Bill Kelly comes to our house for his dinner every working day. It coincides with my break from school – what we now call a lunch break, but then it was dinnertime. Bill's great passion is the game of draughts and I am inevitably drawn into regular battle with him on the chequered board. I am a novice. He is unbeatable, but he continues to offer me 'a crack at the title'. He has picked up that phrase from boxing champion Joe Louis – 'I'll give anyone a crack at the title'. I try my best but the blacksmith remains undefeated – champion of Quinn's Kitchen, if not the world. His grip on the title is as tight as the mighty vice in his forge. I trudge back to school. Someday …

And then it happened – on a strange, bleak day. Could it have been a Good Friday? Outside, a foul-smelling stray billygoat roams the street. I watch intently as the soot-wrinkled hand moves the pieces in an effort to entrap me. But today, something magical happens. I escape the champion's grasp and build up a wall of kings. I win! Bill is dumbfounded.

'Ah, it was that oul' billygoat that distracted me,' he moans.
I put the pieces carefully away. Bill shuffles out the door.
'Never mind, Bill,' I call after him. 'Tomorrow, I'll give you a
crack at the title!'

34 Townlands

And the little townlands all around
I sing the music of their sound –
Muchwood, Glack, the Hill of Down,
Portlester, Shanco and Carronstown –
    Oh goodnight Ballivor, I'll sleep in Trim.

There is indeed music in the names of the townlands. Most of them are corruptions of the original Irish names, but their anglicised forms are mostly pleasant on the ear also. There is history in these names but establishing their true derivation is a minefield – best left to professional scholars. It is worth listing them for the music of their names alone. The following list suggests their derivation also, but in many cases one can only speculate. Some historical footnotes are also included.

Ballinadrimna – *Druimne* is a little ridge, so this is probably the town of the little ridge.
Baskinagh – *Baiscne* is an old Irish word for a tree, so this refers to a wooded place.
Batterstown – *Baile an Bhóthair*, the town of the road.
Carronstown – Origin obscure. Thomas Poynton from Carronstown was the first Catholic layman to emigrate to New Zealand in 1828.
Cloncarneel – *Cluain chairn aoil*. Possibly the meadow of the lime heap?

Cloneycavan – The meadow of the hollow place? Home of Cloneycavan Man – the two-thousand-year-old skeleton found in the bog.

Cloneygrange – *Gráinseach*, anglicised to grange, means a granary, so – the meadow of the granary?

Cloneylogan – Another meadow. Logan's meadow?

Cloughbrack – *Cloch bhreac*, the speckled stone. Site of a Mass Rock.

Coolronan – Ronan's corner.

Corballis – *Corrbhaile*, the odd town …

Crossanstown – Origin obscure.

Derryconnor – *Doire* – the oak wood of O'Connor.

Donore – *Dún Uabhair*, the fort of pride. Site of a Dominican abbey, which had a boarding school in the seventeenth century.

Glack – A hollow place. Site of a Mass Rock.

Killaconnigan – The church of Conaghan? The ruined church of St Kinneth stands in the cemetery.

Killballivor – Original name of the village, in the parish of Killaconnigan.

Kilmer – Possibly a corruption of *Coill Mhór*, the Big Wood. cf. the nearby Muchwood.

Moyfeigher – *Máigh* is a plain. Possibly the wooded plain.

Moyrath – *Maigh Ratha*, the plain of the rath or fort.

Muchwood – self-explanatory!

Parkstown – the town of the fields.

Portan/Portown – *Port na hAbhann*, the bank of the river (Boyne).

Portanob – *Port na n-Ab*, the bank (raised earthwork) of the abbots. Site of an early monastic school.

Portlester – Bank of the vessel? Site of a victorious battle by Owen Roe O'Neill, 12 September 1643. Remnants of his army are said to have settled in Coolronan.

Rathcormick – *Rath Chormaic*, Cormac's fort.

Rathkeenan – Another rath or fort.

Robinstown – Origin obscure.

Shanco – Possibly *sean-chuach*, the old hollow. Home of the tennis club, set up by a group of enthusiasts in the 1940s and subsequently an important sporting and social venue.

35 The Balladeer

Every village has – or should have – a balladeer, a local chronicler of important events such as football victories, a new industry, the coming of electricity or television. It is a continuation of the old oral tradition when historic events were set down in song or verse and the story was passed on through the generations. Ballivor was lucky in having Tom Kiernan of Carronstown as its balladeer.

Tom was affectionately known as 'Tiddley-aye-dil-dum'. Master Conway would boast that he taught many doctors and engineers but only one poet. There was a ballad tradition in the Kiernan family. I set down here three examples of Tom's artistry. I am indebted to the late Jimmy Murray, who sang them for me in McLaughlin's bar in the course of making the radio documentary *Goodnight Ballivor, I'll Sleep in Trim* in 1995.

1. 'The Ballivor Football Song'

This commemorates Ballivor's first major football trophy – winning the Meath Intermediate Championship in 1948 by beating Trim. This song has been heard all over Europe, thanks to Medhbh Conway, who had it as her 'party piece' at every European Broadcasting Union meeting she attended over a long career. Tom Kiernan had been a substitute on the Ballivor Junior team when it played its first match on 30 March 1930.

1.
We have football teams in Kerry
    And football teams in Clare
A football team in Galway
    And another in Kildare
A football team in Cavan
    The second out of none
But if they meet the Ballivor boys
    There's bound to be some fun.

2.
For down here in Ballivor
    We have fifteen gallant youths
Who don their colours white and red
    And fifteen pairs of boots
And then they take the playing pitch
    Like an army going to war
And if you listen for a while
    I'll tell you who they are.

3.
You have Garry down from Crossanstown
    He does defend the sticks
He's very like the 'Mousey' Brown
    With all his little tricks.
He gets down on his hunkers
    And leps up in the sky
And the ball must be a rasper
    If it's going to pass him by.

4.
Another man upon the team
    He's well-known as the Black
He's counted a real stonewall
    When kicking as a back.
He's proved his worth with Rathmolyon

He was the star that day
And afterwards when playing Trim
    He played on famous Fay.
He is as good a half-back
    As ever could be found
And if he lived in Cavan
    He'd be on the Polo Grounds.

5.

And then we come to Dargan
    Who plays a noble part
For every time he gets the ball
    He presses it to his heart.
He dodges his man and gets away
    Like a bullet from a gun
And up along the sideline
    He'll do his solo run.
And if he is re-captured
    He does a simple thing
He kicks the ball to Dempsey
    Who's on the other wing.

6.

Now Dempsey is another man
    On this Ballivor team
And from his early schooldays
    On football he was keen
Some players try to shun him
    But it only goes to show
His name was champion with the gloves
    Fifty years ago.

7.

Paddy Dixon at the centrefield
    Who kicks the hour through
He was the instigation

Of Young Ireland's Waterloo
He kicks upon the county
    And of him we should be proud
He should be in the half-back line
    When Meath were kicking Louth.

8.
He's backed up at centrefield
    By a lad named Andy Clarke
A youth of only eighteen years
    And as lively as a lark.
He gets his ball and kicks it
    And of no man he finds blame
He's the only man upon the team
    Who has a double name.
9.
You've read in daily papers
    The names of some great men
The games they play, the balls they stop
    And how and where and when.
But the man that brought Ballivor
    To the point just where they are
His name is Tommy Daly
    And he's from the Central Bar.

10.
Mick Reilly and Pat Rispin
    Put in some lovely work
But the toughest man upon the team
    Is a man they call Pop Burke.
When Pop is on the playing pitch
    He's out to do or dare
He's the only man upon the team
    That has always doctor's care.

11.
With Dixon, Doyle and Regan
    You have the inside three,
Paud Conway on the forty yards
    To take the close-in free.
He puts his hand up to his head
    And brushes back his hair
And every time he kicks the ball
    He lobs it in the square.

12.
One more before I finish
    I'm sure you will agree
He is one Father Dowling
    And he's gone across the sea.
He's gone to play another game
    Upon a foreign sod
And every goal he scores o'er there
    He wins a soul for God.

13.
So now to conclude and finish
    I wish for to relate
Ballivor were the champions
    In nineteen-forty-eight.
And if they pull together
    And have no team they will fear
They will have a famous senior team
    All in the coming year.

NOTES
Verse 3: The 'Mousey' Brown had played in goals for Meath in earlier
    years.
Verse 4: The 'Black' was Tom 'Black' Doyle (to distinguish him from Tom
    'White' Doyle and Tom 'Red' Doyle). The Polo Grounds, New York,
    was the venue for the 1947 All-Ireland Final.

Verse 6: Dempsey was Michael Dempsey, father of Noel Dempsey T.D. The 'champion with the gloves' was the boxer Jack Dempsey.

Verse 7: Ballivor had beaten 'Young Ireland' (Peter McDermott's team) in an earlier round.

Verse 8: It can now be revealed that 'Andy Clarke' was an illegal player. His real name was Jack Lynch (no – not that one) – hence the reference to a 'double name'.

Verse 9: The Central Bar was Walsh's public house.

Verse 10: 'Pop' Burke worked for Dr O'Reilly, hence the reference to the 'doctor's care' …

Verse 13: Trim objected to Ballivor over 'Andy Clarke' but the Leinster Council declared that 'Ballivor were the champions of 1948' (and proper order too!)

2. 'The Bord na Móna Song'

When Bord na Móna began operations in Ballivor after World War II it was a major event for the village. In 1948 Tom Kiernan commemorated the event in song.

1.
You have heard of new inventions
And lots of them you've seen,
The aeroplane, the wireless
The bomb and submarine;
And on the greyhound racing track
You've seen the 'puss' and dog,
But have you seen the new machine
Down in Coolronan bog?

2.
It was in the springtime of the year
This new machine came down;
Some say it came from Berlin
Some say from London town.
More say it came from ould Kildare
From the Bog of Carbury,
But now its in Coolronan
In a place called Derraghlea.

3.
It wasn't long in Coolronan
Till the headman, he came down,
He placed a young man over it
And he called him Captain Brown.
He said 'You are the man in charge
So come and sign the sheet.
But you must supply the company
With ten thousand tons of peat'.

4.
So the Captain gave his signature
And then took full control
Saying 'I will do my utmost
To keep out imported coal.
I'll hire all the local men
That will work early and late
And the young men from Ballivor
They won't have to emigrate'.

5.
It was a short time after
The news it went around –
A job was starting on the bog
Controlled by Captain Brown.
The names of the men would be taken
Up to a certain date
And the supervisor of the job
Was a Mister E. Filgate.

6.
It was early the next morning
Visibility was good.
A man could see to Ballinahee
And back to Cooney's Wood.
And over at Charlie Reilly's

A lorry could be seen –
It was heading for Coolronan
With the second turf machine.

7.
The Captain he was waiting
And the supervisor too,
Saying 'This machine that's coming,
We'll call it Number Two.
We'll send it up the far drain
It's there we'll get dry land,
And from the crowd of working men
We'll pick a good chargehand'.

8.
So they picked out Blondie Byrne
Saying 'I think he'll suit us great –
He was always interested
In getting fire for the State.
And also Patrick Brannelly –
At that work he was keen
And I think we'll try and place him
Over Number One machine'.

9.
The morning of the day arrived
When the work it was to start.
The working men assembled
From every art and part.
A knapsack on the shoulder
Of each working man was seen
And they placed them in a little hut
Beside the turf machine.

10.
The Captain was preparing
While the men were taken on.

He cleaned the carburettor
And a fan belt he put on.
He started up the engine
And away it went – tut! tut!
And by six away that evening
Sixty thousand tons were cut …

11.
It was a short time after
This machine-won turf was dry;
To get it to the harbour
The company did try.
At last they were successful
After many weary weeks,
They had it on the Old Bog road
In large and well-made reeks.

12.
A rumour it was going round
That the turf was up for sale.
The company would sell it
By lorry load or rail.
On the thirty-first of October
An advertisement thus ran:
'Machine-won turf in Coolronan bog
At thirty-nine and six a ton.'

13.
So the lorries came from every part
To bring the turf away
As far as County Cavan
Ballyhaise and Ballybay,
From Navan, Kells and ould Dundalk
Mullingar and down to Street
And over half of Ireland
Went the Bord na Móna peat.

14.
The people of Meath and Westmeath
Of Cavan and of Louth –
Of this *Bord na Móna* company
I'd say they should be proud.
For on a cold and wintery night
In rain and snow and sleet
Sure they can have a fire
Of this *Bord na Móna* peat.

15.
So good luck unto the Captain
And the supervisor too,
To Brannelly and Blondie –
Two workmen good and true –
Who kept those machines going
While the summer sun shone bright
And left us with a lock of turf
For the cold, cold winter's night.

NOTES
Verse 1: Tom Kiernan always referred to the hare as 'puss'.
Verse 3: Captain Brown was the late Jim Brown, also known as 'The Major', who married Isabella Hamilton.
Verse 5: Mr E. Filgate came to the Board in 1946. He was from Co. Louth, and later worked as a salesman for Roadstone.
Verse 8: 'The Blondie' Byrne and Paddy Brannelly were two timber men. They cut down a lot of the beech trees around the lodge. Very fine hardy fellows.
Verse 11: The harbour. The bog was a swamp – a sea of mud – and the harbour represented dry land or a docking place. Nowadays it would be called the 'tip head'.
Verse 12: The old bog road was down at Keoghs'. Thirty-nine and six – 39 shillings and sixpence. In the early years of *Bord na Móna* in Ballivor, there were a lot of ex-Army men such as Peter Campbell. Discipline was very strict – it was run on army lines – hence the title 'Captain Brown' too.

3. 'The Feis Cup Song'

In 1950 further honours came to Ballivor when they beat Donoughmore in the Feis Cup Senior Football final. Once again, Tom Kiernan was on hand to chronicle the great day.

1.
The 23rd of November being the date of the year
To get over to Navan we all did appear
An IOC bus sure it soon brought us o'er
To play out the Final against ould Donoughmore.

2.
That day over Navan the sun it did shine
The crowds they flocked in from each side of the Boyne
From Trim up to Dublin, from that to Rathcore
Dunshaughlin, Dunsany, Dunboyne and Donore.

3.
From Scrugán to Scrugscoop [?] and out to Girrock
Athboy and Sheecore [?] aye and down near Shercock
From the hills of Oldcastle to the Gap of Dunleer
Sure they all turned out for the game of the year.

4.
So Ballivor dressed up in the white and the red
With Dixon their captain right there at their head
He said, 'Come on boys now, our bones will be sore
Before we are finished with this Donoughmore'.

5.
We have Boland and Morgan and Doran – that's three
And another great man that they call Jackie May
And if we pull together and bottle them up
Well it's fifty to one that we'll win the Feis Cup.

6.

And if that we win it, I guarantee you
We will fill it tonight with the ould mountain dew
We'll ate and we'll drink till our backbones do swell
And we'll have a good night down in Crinion's Hotel.

7.

Three thousand spectators and the pitch lookin' fair
Paul Russell, the ref, pegged the ball in the air
And all of the crowd gave a mighty big roar:
'Come on Ballivor, come on Donoughmore!'

8.

It wasn't long started till Ballivor did press
A goal it was scored in five minutes or less
From that to the finish it was score after score
Went up in abundance against Donoughmore.

9.

One of the spectators stood out on his own
He came from Ballivor and his name was McKeown
His cap and his coat they went up so high
That people round Navan seen them in the sky.

10.

So now to conclude, I have no more to say
The cup's in Ballivor for a year and a day.
And when next year comes and we hand it o'er
I hope 'twill be won back by ould Donoughmore.

NOTES
Verse 1: IOC (Irish Omnibus Company?) was a transport company of the
   time.
Verse 3: Scrugán and Girrock (*Cnoc na nGiorria* – the hill of the hares)
   are districts in the bog. The origins of Scrugscoop and Sheecore are
   obscure.
Verse 6: Crinion's Hotel stood in Market Square, Navan.

36 The Things They Said

This is just a random recollection of expressions and 'turns of phrase' I recall from my childhood. Many of them may not be peculiar to Ballivor or even to Meath, but all of them are part of the richness, colour and individuality of the speech of rural Ireland at that time.

'Goodnight Ballivor, I'll sleep in Trim.' Origin unknown. Said to refer to a visitor who was refused accommodation in the village after a day's drinking. Some have suggested that 'Trim' refers to the County Home.

'Will you be back?' was usually answered with *'Isn't it cool?'* Inexplicable!

'Nobber Agin The Globe': Jim Crosby's war cry.

'You'll follow a crow for that some day': my father's warning on wasting food.

'Thanks be to God we lived so long and did so little harm': a saying beloved of my mother.

'I'll bring you a lock of blocks, Sergeant': timber-man Norman Pratt's promise (with a pronounced Meath drawl!)

'Gouta that' or *'Golang [long] outa that'*, i.e. away with you!

Three from Johnny Kelly:
'I was so hungry I could eat the sock of a plough.'
'My ancestors were put out on the soft side of the road', i.e.
they were evicted.
'That's the real ass's milk', i.e. the real thing.

'Up Drumlargan. Sin é!' Frank Owens' war cry (or was it his
brother Jack?)

'Feck the ould farmers!' – also attributed to the Owens
brothers.

'T.E. [Potterton, Auctioneer] will take care of all.'

'As contrary as a bag of cats.'

'You can see the cock's step in the evening': a reference to
increasing daylight in springtime.

'Short and sweet, like an ass's gallop.'

'He wasn't within an ass's roar of the place.'

'He couldn't kick snow off a rope.'

'They kicked the lard out of us.'

'You're as thick as a double ditch.' The riposte was: *'You're as
thick as a double ditch, with the Boyne in between!'*

'Hould your hoult!', i.e. hold on a minute.

'Hould your whisht', i.e. shut up!

'He *hot* [hit] me an awful *belt* [blow].'

'Take a running jump at yourself' or 'Take a long walk on a short pier', i.e. get lost!

'The sun was *splittin'* the stones.'

'Isn't it *odious* [extremely] hot?'
'*Fierce* entirely. It'd put a fierce *drouth* [thirst] on you.'

'I ran off but he *cotch* [caught] me and *brang* [brought] me back again.'

'Is your father *ihdin* [inside]?'
'No. He's *abrant* or *beyont* [beyond] in the field.'
'I thought I seen him *adove* [above] at the bridge.'

'He stood *forninst* [opposite] the door with a bag of spuds under his *oxter* [arm].'

'He's as dull as ditchwater.'

'She's very pass-remarkable.'

'She was like a hen on a hot griddle.'

'He gave me an awful *reading* [telling off].'

'He has a power of money, but he wouldn't give you the time of day.'

'He's *snaggin'* *turmits* [turnips] down in the *slangs* [hollows].'

'If you don't stop *peggin'* [throwing] them stones, I'll give you a *puck* in the *gob*!'

'He was going like the hammers of hell.'

'It's only a hen's race to her house.'

'He's the two ends of a hoor!', i.e. he's a right brat.

'You melt [disgusting person], you!'

'Have you e'er a match? I have ne'er a one.'

'I haven't a stitch to wear.'

'There wasn't a stim of light.'

'There's no call [need] for that.'

'He's out cutting thristles [thistles].'

'I'm famished with the cowld [cold].'

'I'd as lief [rather] stand in the rain.'

'I disremember [forget] that day.'

'He's poorly [not well].'

'He's bravely [well].'

'That's only be-the-way' or 'That's all my eye' or 'That's only as-I-roved-out', i.e. that's all made up.

'That table is a bit bockety [unsteady].'

'Give us a slug [drink] of that.'

'He's goin' round with a puss on him like a wet Sunday', i.e. he's in a sulk.

'He's after haivin', i.e. he led with a trump at cards.

'She's an able lassie.'

'He's no daw [fool].'

'He came in unbeknownst to us all', i.e. unnoticed.

'They came from all arts and parts.'

'Put the winkers [blinkers] and the britchin [harness] on the horse and hitch him to the dray [cart].'

'Did you dress [make] the bed?'

'He's a right gobbaloon' or *'a total eejit.'*

'I wouldn't like to disoblige him', i.e. let him down.

'I daar [dare] you.' The riposte was *'I double daar you!'*

'He was bullin', i.e. raging mad.

'The higgler [egg-dealer] is coming today.' (The higgler was the famous Meath footballer, Peter McDermott, the 'Man in the Cap.')

'Lat that ball', i.e. put it over the bar.

'He notched a major and two minors in the second moiety', i.e. he scored a goal and two points in the second half (very much *Meath Chronicle* reporting!)

'The chimley [chimney] is smoking. Open the windie [window] and let a draught in.'

'He frykened (frightened) the life out of me.'

'He's a horrid (or shockin') [awfully] nice fella. He's after axing [asking] me out.'

'Goodnight Ballivor, you're a stirrin' village!'

37 Fair Day

The barricades went up the night before. Stout planks resting on an assortment of barrels protected each house from the invading hordes. There would be occasional improvisations with ladders, wheelbarrows, old gates or doors. In some instances windows were boarded up. As dusk fell, the village resembled a film set of a Western, where the townspeople anxiously awaited the arrival of a notorious gang.

> *On fair days for a few bob we minded cattle*
> *And looked important with ashplant and prattle.*
> *A deal was done with the slapping of hands*
> *And we bought Peggy's Leg from McGovern's van.*
> *Oh goodnight Ballivor, I'll sleep in Trim.*

The fair was held on 17 April and 29 October each year on the village street, hence the barricades. Lying in bed as dawn broke I could hear the early arrivals – the rattle of hooves on the tarred road, the collective breathing of tiring animals who had been driven quite a distance. 'Hup! Hup!' 'Get back outa that!' The angry cry of the drover was accompanied by the thwack of an ash plant across an animal's flank. It was important to get a prime 'stand' for your animals, to catch the eye of passing dealers. I leaped out of bed with anticipation. Fair Day meant not only a day off school but an opportunity to earn money minding the cattle.

The street filled up rapidly. Clusters of yearling cattle here, older restive bullocks there, with the occasional animal making a dart for freedom, slithering on the fouled street and causing minor mayhem before being cornered and hooshed back to its stand. A huddle of nervous sheep, a creel of bonhams, one of whom emits ear-splitting shrieks as he is hauled out of the creel by the hind leg for closer inspection. The growing cacophony hurried me through breakfast. I pulled on my wellingtons and retrieved the stout ashplant I had already secreted for this day.

It was important to look knowing and serious and confident as I worked my way down the street, offering my services as a 'minder'. There would be refusals but eventually a job was landed.

> *Keep a close eye on them now, young fellow – especially on that big black fellow in the corner. He's a holy terror. I'm telling you I'll be glad to see the back of him!*

So I marched up and down trying to look in control. Occasionally I would lean on my stick, aping the posture of my seniors, now and then administering a smart slap to the rump of one of my charges – just to let them know who was in control. And all the time eyeing the big black fellow in the corner, inwardly terrified that he might make a bolt for freedom.

It was an exhilarating experience to be caught up in the growing frenzy as dealers came by, made inspections, asked a price and walked away in laughter, only to be called back and asked to make an offer. The haggling followed.

> *'I'd be giving them away at that price.'*
> *'Ye'll not get better from me.'*
> *'I sold two of them last week for ten pound more.'*
> *'Well you should've sold them all 'cos that's crazy money to be askin …'*

The banter occasionally got heated and tempers rose until a 'tangler', a middle-man, would mysteriously intervene and invite buyer and seller to 'split the difference' and attempt to slap their hands together in a deal. Sometimes it worked, sometimes not – when the dealer barged away through the onlookers in a huff.

I stood there, oblivious of the dung that was now streaming down the street and spattering poorly protected housefronts. Oblivious too of the fetid smells that filled the air and of the general discomfort that was added to by the inevitable rain. This was life – real and throbbing with excitement.

The Ballina bus inched its way through the steaming animals. Inside, the passengers peered out, bemused, at the chaos that was unfolding in the street. Now and then a skidding wheel sprayed cowdung over us cattle people. We laughed dismissively as we made half-hearted attempts to brush it off. The morning wore on and the novelty of cattle-minding wore off. Ideally my boss would make a sale by lunchtime and pay me off (handsomely, I hoped) so that I could then turn to Danny McGovern's van. Danny came from Athboy each fair day to set out his stall of sweets such as Peggy's Leg and bullseyes, fruits and enticing trinkets.

What I did not want to witness was my boss disappearing into the Greyhound Bar, where he would bemoan the abysmal cattle trade and forget about his cattle – and me. The worst thing of all to happen was when a particularly irate Fr Cuffe, finding himself without altar boys for ten o'clock Mass, marched out to the street, muttering something about God and Mammon, and hauled me into the church, telling me I was both a curmudgeon and a rapscallion. On that particular occasion I was a penniless curmudgeon.

The day wore on. Hunger pangs set in. Legs grew weary. The big black fellow threw a challenging look in my direction. And the dung. Everywhere the dung. Please let there be a sale soon. Once, in a desperate attempt to stave off hunger, Mickey Fagan and I nicked a bag of oranges from under Danny McGovern's van – only to discover that the oranges were all rotten. Vengeance is mine, saith the Lord.

But inevitably, thankfully, a sale would materialise. A shiny half-crown was pressed into my palm.

'Good young fellow! Ye did well!'

I shook my ashplant triumphantly at the big black fellow in the corner and made my way to Danny McGovern's van for some serious legitimate business. Later there would be recriminations when I made my way home to face my mother.

'Look at the state of you! Get those clothes off you at once ...' But for now there would be indulgence. Fair day also provided an opportunity for my mother's entrepreneurial skills. She cooked and served dinners for hungry dealing men.

The noise in the street abates. A few pathetic cattle low with hunger and fatigue. The barricades start to come down. Pathways and channels are sluiced down. The pubs are thronged as deals are celebrated. There is raucous merriment. My father will be busy tonight.

38 The Names They Had

As with all communities, Ballivor abounded with nicknames. In the main they were not malicious, but acute observations of character, talent or physical traits. They were applied affectionately – in the main. It is with equal affection that I have assembled them in verse, with the help of the collective memory of some Ballivor natives. In making this collection I discovered for the first time that my father was known as 'the Skipper'. It could have been worse ...

> 'Mixer' Dixon went to England
> But 'Stonewall' stayed at home.
> 'The Pope' lived in the Central Bar
> And not in Holy Rome.
>
> 'The Major' Brown lived in our town.
> His brother was 'The Jeezer' Jack,
> And 'The Whirley' Reilly met a German spy
> Who fell out of the sky in Glack.
>
> We had in all three Tom Doyles –
> A 'Black', a 'White' and a 'Red' or *Rua*,
> And Mr L'Estrange of Les Boco Stores
> Was just 'Jabok' to me and you.

'Nanto' Cunningham wed the 'Foxy' Ryan
And they lived up Muchwood way
While 'The Cruice' Owens raised his glass
And roared 'Up Drumlargan, Sin é!'

'The Pinkeen' Dargan ran a sizeable farm
'The Darkie' Miggin drove a hackney car.
'The Twinny' Byrne gave Fox's Mints to Christian and to pagan
'O 'tis sir, 'tis sir, 'tis sir' said 'the Tissir' Fagan.

Not alone did we have three Tom Doyles, we had three Neddy Duignans – Big Neddy, Young Neddy (Big Neddy's son) and Little Neddy. We had two Kit Miggins – the 'Black' and the 'Redser'. And even if you were the only holder of the name, any distinguishing characteristic had to be recognised. Hence Andy Bligh was *always* known as Big Andy Bligh …

'Ginger' Owens had jet-black hair
While 'the Towney' Fagan had a London air
'Spider' Kelly to the GAA was true
And 'the Giant' Dunne was five feet two.

'Sugarstick' Garry was as nice as pie
While 'Arugah!' was Tom Crosby's cry
'The Bowler' Reynolds hit sixes and fours
And 'Jaykers' McLaughlin ran the General Stores.

'The Showman' Kelly had quite a swagger
'The Farmer' McKeown was a turnip-snagger
Christy Fleming hurled as sweet as a fiddle
But why was he called 'Jam in the Middle'?

'Crash' Corrigan had one hour of football glory
And 'What's the News' Leech was on the story

'The Geanc' Dempsey's nose was truncated
And guess where Dick 'Minaulty' originated?

'The Skipper' Quinn enforced the law of the land
And 'Tar-barrels' Kearney was his next in command
But stand aside 'Skipper' and 'Tar-barrels',
'The Big Man' in town was Father Patrick Farrell ...

39 In Sickness and in Health

On Thursday, 11 December 1941, Mrs Hiney grabbed her midwife's bag and hurried up the street to Sergeant Quinn's house to assist Mrs Quinn in her fourth 'confinement'. Later that night she welcomed into the war-torn world (Pearl Harbour had been bombed four days earlier) a fine lump of a boy who now belatedly acknowledges her part in his safe delivery.

Elizabeth Hiney (née Tuite) was a truly remarkable woman. She served as midwife for the Ballivor–Kildalkey area for forty-three years (1919–1962) and as such would have delivered hundreds of babies – two entire generations. Her first delivery is said to have been Master Barney Eivers, who would later become our resident veterinary surgeon. It is to our collective shame that her story has never been publicly chronicled. Anecdotes remain. Delivering the child of a traveller woman in a haybarn, where the only swaddling cloth to wrap the infant was the midwife's own apron … a truly Bethlehemic experience. On another occasion she stayed with a mother for three days, surviving on tea alone, knowing that to accept food in a poverty-stricken house would deprive others of a basic subsistence. It is further to our shame that this woman's devoted service to her community has never been publicly acknowledged, apart from a plaque that exists somewhere in the modern health centre (the old national school). We can do better, surely.

Once we had arrived into the world, our health largely depended on the care and nutrition of the home. Such care and nutrition depended on family circumstances. There was a lot of poverty about and wartime food rationing was an added problem. Vitamin deficiency led to rickets. Infectious diseases such as diphtheria, rheumatic fever, whooping cough, mumps, measles, tuberculosis (TB) and infantile paralysis (polio) were every parent's nightmare. The latter two diseases in particular could ravage a family (see *The Little Black Book*). Our local doctor was Thomas Lynch, who was based in Athboy. He held a dispensary clinic twice weekly in Ludlow's house. Dr Arthur O'Reilly from Portlester also helped out. The dentist, Mr Thornton, was also based in Athboy and he held clinics in Hiney's sitting room. Suffice to say that a visit to the dentist was a much-dreaded experience in those days.

There was a school medical service of sorts. Every three years the doctor would visit the school, give diphtheria injections, examine sight and hearing, measure height and weight and refer children for treatment if necessary, as – in my own case – for tonsilectomy. My abiding memory of that procedure is of waking up in bed in Navan Hospital with a basin of blood beside me. The dentist also came to the school and – I am told – performed extractions on the spot (in the master's chair?). Thankfully I have no abiding memories of such procedures.

Our parents administered such potions and lotions as they could – with an admixture of bribes (a Rolo!) and threats for the particularly nasty medications such as Milk of Magnesia (for stomach upsets) or Castor Oil or the dreaded senna (to regularise the bowels). These barbarities became available when Hugh Gunn opened his pharmaceutical emporium in December 1944. Here too were tonics such as Buckfast Tonic Wine and jars of malt (a distinctly treacle-like substance) to help us recover from debilitating ailments. Elsewhere you could buy 'medicinal stout' in small (one-third of a pint) bottles and mix it with milk in the hope of making it palatable. In the Quinn household the tried and trusted tonic was an egg-flip – a beaten egg added to warm milk, with a dash of sherry. At least it was pleasantly palatable, unlike the much-vaunted raw egg which I could never contemplate, much less swallow.

Outside of the formal and approved medical system there were lots of 'cures', either held by gifted people or handed down through the generations as folk cures, often bound up with religious practices. Mrs Lacey of Killyon had a cure for ringworm – a skin disease often contracted by children through contact with cattle. The root of the buttercup was washed, chopped and fried in unsalted butter. The resulting paste was applied to the infected area. Paddy Cunningham (father of footballer Bertie) had a cure for warts, whether on man or beast. You simply had to count the warts and agree to pray for Paddy each night and he would pray for you. Mrs Lacy favoured rubbbing nine ivy leaves on the wart while Mrs Jordan of Coolronan preferred dandelion milk.

Frank Dempsey – postman, blacksmith and grandfather of Noel, T.D. – had a cure for sprains through prayer and a rubbing of the injured area. Mrs Jordan had two cures for a stye in the eye – a common infection in days past. You could apply cold tea leaves to the stye, or take a gooseberry thorn and point it (carefully!) nine times at the stye before throwing it away. Many of these cures were accompanied by simple prayers such as 'In the name of the Father and of the Son and of the Holy Ghost, Amen'. An invocation to stop bleeding was commonly used –

> *Our Saviour was born in Bethlehem*
> *And christened in the Jordan*
> *The water being clear*
> *The water being good*
> *As our Saviour passed by*
> *The water stood*
> *By His power*
> *And in His name*
> *I command this blood*
> *To do the same.*

Common herbs used as remedies included garlic (for digestion and colds), marjoram (toothache), lemon balm (exhaustion), mint (repelling fleas and preventing milk from curdling), parsley (bad breath), sage (mouthwash) and tarragon (dog bites).

(For the above information on folk cures I am indebted to the children of Coolronan National School, who gathered such information in a 1980s project under the guidance of Maureen McGearty, N.T.)

Outside the parish there were many reputed healers, the best-known of whom was the Dunboyne herbalist Sean Boylan (father of the Meath football manager and current herbalist, Sean). I recall my father bringing my uncle John from Monaghan to Dunboyne for 'a bottle' for his stomach condition.

Many of the folk cures were equally applicable to animals. Before the advent of a resident veterinary surgeon, Joe Conlon was the man to provide cures for animals – potions which included stout, treacle and mustard.

Many cures and remedies were based on little more than simple faith and the power of prayer. When a visiting priest was asked to pray over Loman Conway's pneumonia, he requested that a subsequent child be called Gerard. Loman's younger brother was named Ultan Gerard Conway. There was also a strong devotion to Saint Brigid. A popular custon was to leave out a scarf or flannel (very much used for 'the pains') on St Brigid's Eve. The saint would duly bless the cloth, giving it curative powers against throat infections, mumps etc. A *piseog* surely, to be laughed at in the twenty-first century?

Well … during Christmas 2007 the daughter of an eminent Ballivor man suffered a bad throat infection, which threatened to prevent her singing with her church choir. Her father produced a sock full of salt which had been 'blessed' on St Brigid's Eve, and instructed his daughter to apply it to her infected throat. She sang like a lark all through Christmas …

I tell the story as it was told to me.

40 The Big Houses

A nineteenth-century topographical dictionary describes the village of Ballivor as 'a pendicle [appendage] of the large and improving estate of the Earl of Darnley'. A mere appendage – thanks a lot, fellows! The Earl donated the sites for both Protestant and Catholic churches. The dictionary notes that there are 'adjoining seats' (i.e. big houses) at Elm Grove and Parkstown.

Elm Grove was the seat of Anthony Browne in the nineteenth century. He was a Catholic landowner who was instrumental (along with the Rickard family) in having the first Catholic church built in the village in the 1830s. He also donated the site for the first Catholic national school in 1864. In the nineteenth century the Catholic bishop would stay at Elm Grove when confirming local children. The original Elm Grove was demolished and replaced by John Quinn (no relation!), who came from the Galway/Clare border in the 1920s. Interestingly, during my childhood Florrie Quinn lived in Elm Grove and was married to the sister of the Bishop of Meath, Dr Kyne. The episcopal link continued! A sister of Florrie's – Celia Lynch – became a TD in the 1950s and was in Leinster House until the 1970s. Her son is the writer Brian Lynch.

Sometime in the 1840s Peter Kiernan (who would become father of our balladeer Tom) lost his right arm as a result of an accident while working at Elm Grove. He was only a boy at the time. To compensate Peter for his loss, Anthony Browne had him educated with his own children. This investment paid off a decade later when the postal system was set up. Because he was literate, Peter Kiernan qualified as our first postman. He would collect the post in Athboy and travel around in his horse and cart delivering it. He blew a bugle at the end of a boreen to let people know of his arrival. In 1867 the Fenian leader James Stephens (known as 'The Wandering Hawk') came to Ballivor and spoke publicly at a local tavern (on the site of McLaughlin's) encouraging people to join his organisation. When Stephens moved on to Athboy, it is said that Peter Kiernan travelled ahead of him with his bugle to warn the Fenian of any possible dangers ... (My thanks to M.J. McGearty for these historical gems!)

Anthony Browne died in 1909 and left his estate to his nephew Jimmy who, sadly, was declared bankrupt only four years later. The Elm Grove lands were eventually taken over and redistributed by the Land Commission. Part of the land was retained as commonage for local people and was known as 'The Cowplot'. (Many a summer evening I was sent up to The Cowplot to bring our two cows 'home' to the barracks for milking.) The quaint cut-stone gate lodge became home to Guard Mitchell and his family. Guard Mitchell and his wife Nora produced fourteen children. How they all managed in that little cottage I will never know, but manage they did.

A final word on Elm Grove. For years we children were mystified and frightened by the 'ghost hand' – a huge 'hand' that was imprinted on a corner of the estate wall. We wondered and worried about the 'ghost' as we passed by on the way to the bog. It wasn't until many years later that I learned it was but a 'sapper's' mark, used in mapping by the Ordnance Survey. How disappointing! The 'ghost's hand' offered much more interesting possibilities.

Of the other 'seats' I have little to relate. Parkstown House, a fine three-storey building facing the Trim Road, was originally the 'seat' of the Parr and Taylor families. In my childhood it was the home of the McKays to which I was invited 'up to play' occasionally and where I could only marvel that the McKays owned *two* wireless sets ... what opulence! Elm Grove and Parkstown are happily still occupied, but sadly the same cannot be said of the third 'big house' – Kilmer House, off the Killyon Road. It was once home of the Montgomery family but today only some of the outhouses and cobbled yards remain.

41   The Words We Used

When in the midst of horseplay in the schoolyard turf shed, a boy might expose his *boidín* (penis) or in a dark corner another boy might smoke *cíob* (turf root) in a *dúidín* (clay pipe) – they were not only being bold, they were also speaking Irish. There were many Irish words living in our daily language. Some still survive, many others have sadly disappeared. Words like *ciotóg*, *garsún*, *smithereens* and *amadán* are common all over the country. Other words are specific to different regions. The late Margaret Conway made valiant efforts to collect and preserve words from South Meath and published various articles on the subject in *Ríocht na Mí* – the journal of the Meath Archaeological and Historical Society. The following lists draw from her work and that of her daughter Medhbh, and from my own memory.

We caught pinkeens *(pincín)* or minnows in the river. On the way home from school we picked and ate sally-cuckoo *(sail na gcuach)* or sorrel from the hedgerow. On the bog we would look for glackeens *(glaicín)* or bilberries and munogues *(múnóg)* – another type of berry. Be careful to stand on a punkawn *(puncán)* – a raised sod – and avoid the soomera *(súmaire)* – a hole in which you would quickly sink. We boiled the poreens *(póirín)* or small potatoes for the hens, and for those who had no hens we collected a cludogue *(clúdóg)* of eggs at Easter (be careful there isn't a glugger *(gliogar)* or bad egg among them!). When sowing seed potatoes you could carry them in a little sack or *práiscín*. A useless fellow might be said to be 'not worth a trawneen' *(tráithnín)* or a straw. A trawneen trissock *(tráithnín triosach)* was a hoar frost. Don't eat a cosha pooka *(caise púca)* or 'puffball' mushroom – it's fairy cheese! When we came across a snail in his shell, we would say – 'Shellemy, shellemy *(seilmide)* pooka, stick out your horns!'

Look at the spawgs *(spág)*, or big feet, on him! He has a dhoor *(dúr)* look on him! What sort of a meeawe *(mí-ádh)* or misfortune befell him? He's a bit of a slieveen *(slíbhín)* or sly, cunning fellow. What stawr *(stáir)* or sulk is on him now? She's a bit of a bawrshock *(báirseach)* or a brawling woman alright! Look at the cut of her – she's a right streel *(straoill)* or untidy woman! God love her – she's only a spidogue *(spideog)*, a robin i.e. a tiny creature.

He's after scrawbin' *(scráb)* or scratchin' my face! He went out to snag *(snag)* or cut the leaves off the turnips. I'm just striggin' *(striog)* the cow i.e. squeezin' the last drop of milk from her. He's full of ould pishogues *(piseog)* or superstitions. He made a proshock *(praiseach)* or mess of the job. There wasn't a screed *(scríd)* or a bit of anything in the house.

In the morning Master Conway might bring in a spreesh *(spríos)* or fire embers to get the fire going and then he would send someone out to the turf shed for a boclawona *(bacla mhóna)* or armful of turf. 'A wirristrue [*A Mhuire is trua* – i.e. O Mary, pity us] – but it's a cold morning,' he might say …

Irish words apart, we had our own names for things. Pissybeds were dandelions. Pismires were ants. Johnny McGorys were haws – which reminds me of a nonsense rhyme –

Will I tell you a story
About Johnny McGory?
Will I begin it?
That's all that's in it!

Breda McLaughlin remembers Tommy Clinton teaching her this –

Dr McGrane fell down a drain
Is he far in? said Biddy Quinn
To the shinbone, said Tommy McKeown
Throw him a rope, said Bobby Hope
Throw him a bun, said Andy Dunne!

To which I can only reply –

Well done, said ould Dunne when young Dunne was
born!

42 Threshing Day

The great juggernaut had lumbered into McLaughlin's Yard while I slept, towed there by a tractor and parked alongside a mountainous stack of cornsheaves. The threshing mill. A *frisson* of excitement ran through the classroom when the distinctive rumble of the mill was heard in the distance. Where is it? Where is it? Dargan's I'd say. No, McKeown's. I hope it's at Jim Newman's. He has lovely apples ... When they were released from school they raced to the threshing scene. Threshing was a community event. It required a *meitheal* – a team of workmen and a back-up team of catering and waiting staff to feed the hungry and thirsty workers. Children were welcome too – to watch and play – and help themselves to the apples when the mill came to Jim Newman's.

The mill must have come to McLaughlin's on a Saturday. I have a clear memory of being present for the entire day's threshing. The mill was an extraordinary presence – a gaudy, misshapen, ungainly giant, now slumbering but about to be woken. I approached it tentatively, fearful that it might snatch me and swallow me into its mysterious innards. The *meitheal* assembles, exchanging greetings and banter.

'I'll go on the bags, Jimmy. Wouldn't be able for the rick this morning.'
'Too much porter last night, I'd say.'

'Had a few scoops alright.'
'Well, in the name of God, we'll make a start.'

A man leaps into the cab of the tractor, now facing the juggernaut. The tractor starts up and slowly the huge belt connecting it to the mill rouses the sleeping monster. Shuddering and juddering it comes to life. It grinds and growls its hunger to the assembled throng. *Feed me*, it cries. *Now!* The *meitheal* springs into action. High up on the rick, two men pitchfork sheaves towards the monster's jaws in an easy, swinging motion. Two other men stand atop the mill. One opens the sheaves with a flashing blade. The other feeds the corn to the monster.

The noise reaches a new level as terrible things happen in the monster's belly.

Then magical things unfold. At one end the giant spews out straw, which is seized upon by two more men who fork it away to make the base of a new rick. At the other end, the grain flies into the bags hooked onto the mill by Jimmy and his friend. The monster is voracious now. He roars and rattles. *More! More! Feed me more!* He is insatiable. The noise is frightening. The belt spins dizzily. Shouts are heard across the din. Now the chaff is flying, choking, blinding and delighting the children who build mounds of it and then dive headlong into it. The whole cacophony is exhilarating – the shouts of the men, the squeals of the children and the relentless rumble and roar of tractor and mill.

Refreshments arrive. Bottles of porter to slake chaff-dry throats. Lemonade for the children. And all the time the work goes on. The rick of sheaves dwindles. The men now have to toss the sheaves aloft. The rick of straw is growing. The sacks of grain are ferried away to the barn. Suddenly the great show stops. Mealtime. Trays and plates of generous doorstep sandwiches, hardboiled eggs, pots of tea. The chaff still swirls as the children play.

'Ah gouta that. Ye have me tae ruined!'

Conversation about football, the weather, politics. Laughter. If the threshing were a day-long event, the men would be summoned to the kitchen for a sit-down meal – a roast of lamb or beef.

Once again a call to action. The fearsome belt drives the monster's appetite into a further frenzy. Now the shouts and screams reach a new intensity. Rats! The pitchfork men try to skewer the rats now desperately trying to escape the remaining sheaves. Those that escape must contend with a local terrier. McGearty's dog Fido is especially welcome at the threshing. Once, at Newman's threshing, Fido killed a record fifty-one rats. I was terrified of rats and would stay well clear of where Fido stood alert, waiting to pounce. Even their sleek brown dead bodies made me shiver. I had nightmares of someone grabbing a rat by the tail and slinging it towards me.

The last sheaf is fed. The monster calms down and returns to slumber. The yard is tidied up.

'Well done, men. Great job!'
'I'll see you so, Jimmy.'
'Good luck so. Good luck.'

Tonight when I am asleep, the juggernaut will creep out of McLaughlin's yard meekly in tow to a chugging tractor. Tomorrow I will return to play in the chaff-hill, fearful that an escaped or injured rat might still be in there, waiting for revenge.

43 Sensations

Lost sounds, smells, tastes, textures ...

The purr of the boiling kettle on the range (from deep in my throat I could mimic that sound perfectly) ... the music of milking as the warm fresh milk sprayed into the rising froth ... the slice and suck of the slane in turfcutting action ... the wheeze of Bill Kelly's bellows and the ring of his anvil ... the empty thwack of the wooden 'clappers' that replaced the altar bell during Holy Week ... the cheeping of 'day-old-chicks' in the aerated box that arrived on the Ballina bus ... the whirring of bicycle wheels as Bord na Móna workers passed through the village early in the morning ... the church clock counting the hours through the night ... the raucous concert of crows settling for the night in the Protestant church grounds ... 'I taut I taw a puddy-tat' on the radio ... 'Tantum Ergo' sung at Benediction ... Ian Priestly Mitchell on the Hospitals' Sweepstakes programme saying 'Goodnight everyone, goodnight'.

The scent of new-mown hay under a hot sun, occasionally sweetened by the honey of a disturbed bees' nest ... lilac in bloom in May ... the fresh smell of rain on the road after a long dry spell ... the all-pervading aroma of leather and wax in my Uncle John's saddlery ... the faintly attractive smell of cowdung and the reassuring warm body odour of cows in their stalls ... the confidence-boosting smell of resin smeared on our palms to absorb the master's slaps ... Master Conway's tobacco ...

heather and pine scents carried on a bog breeze ... an open turf fire ... 'Vicks' rubbed on your chest when colds attacked ...

The taste of a ripe, red *robbed* apple ... Peggy's Leg and liquorice pipes ... the bitter tang of sloes that clung like fur to the roof of your mouth ... the luxuriant sweetness of mother's apple tarts and rice puddings ... wild mushrooms sat on the hob with a sprinkle of salt and a knob of butter ... the rich crispness of new-fallen hazelnuts ... steaming hot new potatoes in melting butter ... sherbet in a lucky bag ... Tate & Lyle's Golden Syrup on bread ... over-ripe gooseberries and blackcurrants ... bittersweet sorrel ('sally-cuckoo') picked from the hedgerow on the way home from school ... long-lasting bullseyes and gobstoppers ... the dreaded castor oil, milk of magnesia and senna liquid ...

The tickling silky touch of my mother's fox fur ... the slippery slime of a frog caught in a summer meadow ... the fiery sting of spring nettles harvested to feed turkey chicks, followed by the balm of spittle-smeared dock leaves ... bare feet stepping on molten tar ... fingers sinking into the cool pulp of a newly cut sod of turf ... hands plunged into icy water to wash potatoes for the pig's pot ... the flaky bristle of a pig's skin ... the rough slobber of a calf's tongue lick.

44 Ballyfin

*In the autumn of 1954 a new chapter of my life began. I went to
boarding school in Co. Laois. Goodnight Ballivor, I'll sleep in
Ballyfin! The following are the opening pages of the script of
the radio documentary* Ballyfin – A Boarding School Memory.
*They are an attempt to capture that traumatic experience – first
night away from home ...*

There was a giant stone bird sitting on either gate pillar. He
would learn later that they were coots, for this was originally
the home of the Coote family. It was now Patrician College,
Ballyfin Demesne, Portlaoise, Co. Laois – a boarding school for
boys. It was September 1954. He was twelve years of age and –
holidays apart – this would be his home for the next five years.
He was fearful. He had left the familiarity and security of home
in a small village in Co. Meath – sixty miles away ...
    The Ford Prefect rattled over the cattle grid – the first time
he had seen a cattle grid. 'Canadian gates' they were called –
and they seemed to clang 'Goodbye' – a goodbye to the village,
goodbye to his friends, his parents, goodbye to the world ...
    The avenue was long, winding out of the autumn sunlight,
into dark woods and then suddenly into the light again. And
there it was – a huge mansion, the biggest he had ever seen.
Four great columns guarded the entrance doors where the
President stood greeting the parents. The brothers wore long
black soutanes with green sashes. He shook hands with the

President, Brother Silverius. He would later learn that the boys
called him 'Punk'. Brother Silverius said he hoped this young
man would be as good as his brother. It was good having a
brother in the school already. It helped in the settling in ...
    They climbed the two flights of stone stairs to the dormitory.
On the first landing were the washroom and toilets. He would
spend many cold winter mornings in the washroom waiting for
a free handbasin for a quick wash before Mass. The dormitory
was on the next landing – a long L-shaped room with fifty or
sixty beds. His brother chose two beds half-way down. The
trunk was opened and the starched sheets with his name sewn
on the corner were procured. They made up the beds and
packed their lockers with clothes and toiletries ...
    The dormitory grew noisier as more boys arrived. Old boys –
anyone in second year or beyond – shouted greetings and
swaggered about knowingly. The new boys tried hard to look
settled and happy and knowing. And then it was time for his
parents to go ... He swallowed hard and said goodbye to his
father. His mother kissed him – he knew she would miss him,
the baby of the family. He fought back the tears and waved
goodbye as the car moved down the avenue, around the bend
and into the woods.
    He awoke to a new and strange world. Brother Angelus
marched through the dormitory ringing a handbell. It was so
unusual to find himself sharing a room with sixty other boys.
The hubbub and clamour grew as the washroom filled up and
boys queued up for handbasins. He washed quickly. The
towel smelled of home. He buried his face in it, wishing that
smell would linger ... His brother told him to hurry. The day
proper began as every day would begin – with Mass in the
Oratory.
    Fr Phelan came in from Ballyfin village to say Mass. The
juniors knelt at the front of the Oratory. He himself was right
under the huge fireplace which was now boarded up. Each seat
had a series of white enamel numbers affixed to it. Later he
would learn how to unscrew the number with a nail file, insert

a message behind the number and screw it back on. In this way he would be remembered in fifty years time, maybe forever ...

He thought of the many times he had served Mass in his home village, the dark winter mornings when the frost pinched his face on the way to the church. He would gladly exchange that for this bright September morning. He wondered what his parents were doing now ... his mother probably at Mass praying for him ... his father stoking the range ... Roy the dog waiting to be released from his kennel. He wished he was at home ...

45 The Leaving

June 1955. I came home from my first year in boarding school. Home. There is warmth in the word. It denotes familiarity, ease and a comfort far removed from the spartan conditions and loneliness of boarding school. Suddenly, however, home was moving. A decision had been taken.

My father was retiring early from An Garda Síochána and we were moving to Dublin. Dublin? What did I know of Dublin? Little enough. An annual visit on December 8th – Clerys Department Store, the Theatre Royal. An occasional visit to Croke Park. Dublin was the Big Smoke, the home of the Jackeens. Far removed from Ballivor – even if it was physically only thirty miles away. I was apprehensive. Oh yes, Dublin would be slick and sophisticated. There would be plush cinemas and theatres. The seaside would be near at hand. There would be fish and chip shops, toyshops, bookshops. Croke Park would be only a bus ride away. On a *doubledecker* bus! Dublin would be the Promised Land. Running water and inside toilets. No more traipsing to the village pump or to the privy down the yard.

But would there be pinkeens in the local river? Would there even be a local river? Would there be orchards to rob? Could you throw water on the street on a frosty night to make a slide? Would there be cattle to mind on fair days? Would there be bonfire nights? Could you go out early on a misty summer morning to pick a hank of mushrooms? Would there be juicy blackberries to gorge yourself with on an autumn evening? Would there be a football pitch up the road? Would there be a Harry Garry to serve you with a joke in the local shop? Or a Bill Kelly to give you a crack at the draughts title? Or a Sean Egerton to practise 'heading duels' with you outside the butcher's shop? Would there be friends and playmates like John Joe Cummins, Betty Dempsey, Maureen McGearty, Seamus Miggin, Breda McLaughlin?

Cavafy has written – *In those fields and streets where you grew up, there you will always live and there you will die ...*

The ghosts of Ballivor would accompany me for the rest of my life. Master Conway would extol the glories of Marseilles. Michael Leddy would eye me suspiciously when I entered his shop (did he know about the stolen truck?). I would argue with my brother over another ball lost over the wall to Mrs Reynolds. Fr Farrell would interrogate me about the seventh commandment (did he know about the collection plate?). Jim Dargan would kick 'skyscraper' points against Ballinabrackey. Joe Brown would sing 'My Little Grey Home in the West' in Kellys' Summerhouse. Tailor Peter Whitty's dark and lonely room would frighten me. And the grounds of the Protestant church would terrify me on a wild winter evening.

There was an auction – a small auction – of house contents. Furniture. The table I had eaten at, over which I had pored during homework sessions, the beautiful oil lamps, the wind-up gramophone with assorted records – Mario Lanza, Sousa Marches. Pack the remainder away and say goodbye to friends. Into the Ford Prefect and down the street. Past the church. *Introibo ad altare Dei.* Maureen McGearty waves. The village pump. The 'Pope' Walsh's pub. Past Dargans, Hineys. There's Jim Crosby – Nobber Agin the Globe! Murtagh's Shop – a sixpenny ice-cream dunked into a glass of lemonade. Last glimpse of Sherrock's Garage. 'Made it Ma! Top of the World!' Cummins' friendly little house. The White Walls. The village recedes through the back window. Look in the mirror. Your parents' eyes are glistening with tears. When have you ever seen

them both cry? This was their home for twenty years. Where
they reared their four children. Where he was The Sergeant. No
more. Don't look back! You must look back. This was Ballivor,
your home for the first fourteen years of your life. And there
you will die.

> And when I come to the end of my days –
> Be it natural causes or nuclear haze –
> My last words will surely be
> (Even if I'm the sole survivor)
> Oh goodnight world, I'll sleep in Ballivor.

46 Envoi

And was there no darkness ever?
Yes there was but –

But?
We didn't know nor –

Nor?
Did we need to know.

So you were protected?
Yes.

And you were cherished?
Yes.

And you were loved?
Yes and yes.

And you were happy in the end of all?
Yes and yes and yes and yes.